FERMENTATION MADE EASY!

Mouthwatering Sauerkraut

MASTER AN ANCIENT ART OF PRESERVATION, GROW YOUR OWN PROBIOTICS, AND SUPERCHARGE YOUR GUT HEALTH

Holly Howe

DISCLAIMER

The material in this guide should be considered informational in nature and has been written for educational purposes only. As the purchaser of this guide, you understand that the author is not a medical professional and that the information in this guide is not intended as a substitute for the medical advice of a licensed physician. The author claims no responsibility for any person or entity for any liability, loss, or damage caused or alleged to be directly or indirectly caused as a result of the use, application, or interpretation of the material contained in this guide. Please consult your physician or other qualified healthcare practitioner for diagnosis or treatment of any medical problem, and before making changes to your current diet. The statements in this book have not been evaluated by the US Food and Drug Administration.

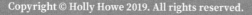

ISBN: 978-1-9990666-0-4
MakeSauerkraut
PO Box 21036
Duncan, BC V9L 0C2
CANADA

PRAISE

"This is the perfect book to lead you directly to sauerkraut happiness and all the digestive and health benefits that come with it. The book is packed, practical, and easy-to-read. Holly Howe is truly the Julia Child of fermentation."

—Health writer Martin Zucker,
co-author of the *Earthing book*

"Just like fermentation can turn a number of simple foods (like cabbage) into a delicious, healthy wonder food, Holly's book will turn even the most basic cook into a fermenting whiz by mastering the art of making sauerkraut. She breaks down a seemingly simple recipe in excellent detail to take all the worry out of learning a new skill – fermenting! Anyone hesitant to try fermenting will benefit from the 'hand holding' advice Holly offers readers as if she were the ancestors of yesterday teaching the next generation this time honored craft."

—Emily S. Kociolek,
owner of Stone Creek Trading, LTD

"Holly Howe has mastered the art of making one of the most beloved and classic ferments, sauerkraut, and explains in-depth how you can too. She thoroughly guides you through the process of kraut making and concludes the book with an impressive selection of mouth-watering sauerkraut recipes. Incredibly detailed and informative book!"

—Stephanie Thurow,
author of *Can It & Ferment It* and *WECK: Small-Batch Preserving*

"Holly's book lives up to its title--her well thought out instructions make fermenting sauerkraut easy and the recipes got my mouth watering! Part 1 is a clear and concise background to the art of fermentation, building a strong case for starting your fermentation adventure with sauerkraut. Part 2 is a thorough preparation, covering the key concepts you need to know and the equipment you will need. I felt part 3 of the book is where we see Holly's years of experience with these 'mighty microbes' come through in well laid-out step-by-step instructions and an easy to understand troubleshooting guide. Finally, parts 4 and 5 build upon that tasty carrot garlic sauerkraut with a dozen straightforward recipes and simple recommendations for incorporating them into your family's meals. Holly's book is a rare balance of just enough art, science and experienced mentorship to give you the confidence to learn and master this important fermented food."

—Christopher Shockey & Kirsten K. Shockey,
authors of *Fermented Vegetables* and *Fiery Ferments*

"Thanks to Holly for sharing her extensive knowledge of the process of fermentation, and for all the wonderful recipes in this book. The mouthwatering palette of sauerkraut recipes are proof enough to the success of her methods, well described in depth, and detail throughout the book. Holly's book empowers us to add more gut-healing fermented food to our diet, which is a good thing."

—Carolyn Herriot, author of *The Zero-Mile Diet Cookbook: Seasonal Recipes for Delicious Homegrown Food* and *A Year on the Garden Path: A 52-Week Organic Gardening Guide*

DEDICATION

This book is dedicated to the trillions of bodacious bacteria that transform simple cabbage into mouthwatering sauerkraut.

WHO THIS BOOK IS FOR

Are you looking for a set of tested and easy-to-follow instructions on how to make your first batch of sauerkraut? Have you tried to ferment sauerkraut but given up due to noxious-smelling results with strange things growing on top? Are you wanting to raise the bar on your current sauerkraut-making process?

Are you wanting to improve your digestion? Has your doctor recommended adding fermented foods to your diet?

If the answer to any of these questions is yes, then this book is for you.

The ancient process of fermentation is undergoing an unlikely resurgence, with products like sauerkraut, kimchi, and kombucha crowding grocery store shelves. With a gentle nudge from the countless articles on the importance of probiotics for gut health, you may start off buying some of these probiotic-rich foods, but soon realize how expensive that becomes and then turn to making your own. However, since most of us did not grow up helping ferment these foods, it soon feels overwhelming trying to find the right recipe and knowing what tools to buy.

In this book, I remove that overload and share my seven steps for successfully fermenting small batches of sauerkraut. My teaching recipe has been refined over the past few years as thousands of readers on my website have put it to the test.

Rest assured, my book will make sure you have the tools and the confidence you need to leave food sitting on your counter for days, if not weeks, as it transforms from salty cabbage into sour sauerkraut. And not only will you find that sauerkraut scrumptious, but you will feel comfortable feeding it to your family and friends.

You'll find more than one favorite recipe in the included set of twenty-one flavorful sauerkraut recipes, and you'll be able to effortlessly add sauerkraut to your diet with my set of serving suggestions. Sauerkraut is more than a topping for hot dogs, and it tastes way better than that canned stuff that comes to mind for most of us.

The recipes are packed with easy-to-find vegetables and seasonings. Outside of possibly a scale for weighing your ingredients, you'll either have what you need at home or have to purchase just a few inexpensive items.

WHAT NOT TO EXPECT FROM THIS BOOK

It is important to know what you should *not* expect out of this book.

This is not an all-encompassing fermentation book. I believe in the power of accomplishing goals or new skills through the power of *one* thing or one place to focus. For fermentation, I believe that one thing is sauerkraut. Due to its low startup costs, readily available supplies, and versatility in ways to consume it, sauerkraut is the perfect *one* ferment to first master. It is then fun and easy to take the basic concepts mastered and apply them to your next ferment.

This is not a recipe book full of recipes that use sauerkraut as a key ingredient. Many jars of flavorful sauerkraut sit at the ready in my refrigerator. When I'm preparing a meal, I pull out a jar, grab a few forkfuls of the probiotic-rich goodness, and place some on my plate, toss it into my salad, top my hamburger with it, swirl some into a bowl of soup, or just eat it right off the fork. I don't complicate my life by having to *make* something with my sauerkraut.

This book does not include directions for canning (heat processing) sauerkraut. I started fermenting sauerkraut as an inexpensive way to add a gut-healing food to my diet. When sauerkraut is heated, the beneficial probiotics and enzymes are lost. I cover suggestions for storage in my teaching recipe.

This book does not cover fermenting sauerkraut in a crock. When making your own sauerkraut in jars with flavor-enhancing ingredients, you'll discover how delicious homemade sauerkraut is. These days, I ferment a good percentage of our family's annual supply of sauerkraut in a stoneware crock. When fermenting in a crock, even greater depths of flavor are unlocked. I recommend you do the same, *after* you've mastered fermenting sauerkraut in a jar. Be patient, learn first how to ferment in a jar, then graduate to fermenting in a crock. I have a teaching recipe for fermenting in a crock on my website. Visit this shortened URL: **fmeasy.me/crock**

WHAT DOES THIS BOOK COVER?

The first chapter clears up the confusion between fermentation, culturing, and pickling, and it explains why fermentation is so safe. It also looks at the importance of the microbial world and why bacteria are so important to the fermenting process.

In chapter 2, I cover the incredible values derived from the fermentation process. Preserving food, making food easier to digest, and making food more flavorful are just a few.

Then, in chapter 3, I cover some of the many ways in which fermented foods can improve your health, all the way from supporting your immune system to weight loss.

Chapter 4 emphasizes the importance of choosing sauerkraut as your first ferment to master, or the next one to master if you are already fermenting other foods.

Next, in chapter 5, I set down a few critical concepts that should not be skipped over. Understanding them helps ensure that you are able to successfully ferment many batches of sauerkraut.

Chapter 6 details three key ingredients for making sauerkraut, one of which you may not guess right off.

Then, in chapter 7, I cover what tools you'll want to gather together for fermenting your first batch of sauerkraut.

In chapter 8, I go hands-on with my Small Batch Fermentation Teaching Recipe. Since this recipe offers extensive tips on all the commonly asked questions, you can jump right to this chapter and get started right away. Then return to previous chapters to gain a better depth of understanding of the process.

Chapter 9 thoroughly covers anything that could go wrong. Fermentation is not an exact science, though I try to make it so, and occasionally a batch may develop mold, smell off, or just not be as crunchy, or soft, as you would like.

Chapters 10, 11, 12, 13 and 14 are where to turn once you have fermented your first batch of sauerkraut using the chapter 8 teaching recipe. Each recipe chapter contains a set of sauerkraut recipes grouped by flavor profile: Simple Sauerkraut Recipes, Savory Sauerkraut Recipes, Sauerkraut Recipes Powered by Beets, Sauerkraut Recipes with a Touch of Sweetness, Sauerkraut Recipes with a Bit of Spicy Heat. Glance over the recipe description and ingredients list to select your next batch of sauerkraut to ferment. There is a wide palette of recipes in those chapters that is sure to please any palate.

Lastly, in chapter 15, I suggest ways to effortlessly add sauerkraut to any meal. Keep things simple and you'll soon find yourself enjoying mouthwatering sauerkraut every day.

Don't forget the afterword: 5 Things I Wish I Had Known Before Embarking on My Fermentation Journey. In addition, you will find the Daily Dosage and Salt Chart in the appendixes handy.

Note: Throughout this book, there are references to valuable outside resources that can be viewed by entering the shortened URL in your browser.

Contents

PART 1

Fermentation: Bacteria at Work

I didn't know it at the time, but I was introduced to the world of fermentation in 2002, when I made my first batch of sauerkraut by following Sally Fallon's recipe for sauerkraut in her book *Nourishing Traditions*. For me, I was making yet another recipe in yet another cookbook. Nothing more. For all it mattered, it could have been a recipe for chocolate chip cookies. I didn't grasp the concept that I was fermenting and that it necessitated the use of our microscopic world. I just knew that all traditional cultures with robust health—as visited and studied in the 1930s by the dentist Weston A. Price—included some type of fermented food in their diets. I wanted that robust health, hence I needed to learn to *make* sauerkraut.

There were no YouTube videos, no websites on fermentation, no cornucopia of must-have fermentation tools on Amazon. In 2002, only Fallon's *Nourishing Traditions* was around to learn the art of fermentation from. Sandor Katz, who describes himself as a fermentation revivalist, did not publish *Wild Fermentation* until a year later; that book is now dubbed "the book that started the fermentation revolution."

As I worked at perfecting my sauerkraut, my kitchen slowly transformed into a wild food lab, and my knowledge of fermentation greatly expanded. In 2007, with the launch of the Human Microbiome Project, a United States National Institutes of Health research initiative to improve the understanding of the microbial flora involved in human health and disease, our knowledge of the impact of fermented foods on our health exploded.

Daily, I'm learning more and more about the incredible value of fermentation, what is happening in the little jar sitting on my counter, and how vital fermented foods are for robust health. I'm honored to have you join me on this journey and not only learn how to ferment sauerkraut, the gateway drug of fermentation, but also develop a deep appreciation for our microbial world.

CHAPTER 1

What Is Fermentation?

Pickles, sauerkraut, sourdough bread, kombucha, and yogurt are all examples of foods that our great ancestors preserved naturally through a process called fermentation. However, one can be easily confused on opening a book on fermentation, grabbing a recipe off the internet, or trying to buy a jar of sauerkraut, and noticing the use of so many different terms: *lacto-fermentation, naturally fermented, cultured, brine pickled, vinegar pickles, quick pickles,* and *refrigerator pickles.*

What do all these terms mean, and which methods of preservation retain all the health benefits you're looking for?

PICKLING VS. BRINE PICKLING VS. CULTURED

Pickling is a general term and refers to the process of preserving foods in an acidic liquid—vinegar, lemon juice, or a naturally created one. When we hear the term *pickle,* most think of that dill pickle spear commonly served alongside a sandwich. Usually, these and other modern day pickles have been pickled with vinegar, which has been heated to sterilize the vegetables and destroy all bacteria—both the beneficial and the pathogenic bacteria. Other terms used to describe this process are *vinegar pickling, quick pickling,* and *refrigerator pickling.*

Brine pickling is both a fermentation method and a pickling method. Instead of adding an acid, like vinegar, to the foods, a salty brine is poured over the vegetables. This causes the bacteria that are naturally present on the vegetables to produce the acidic medium—lactic acid—that gives the pickles their sour flavor and naturally preserves them. Beneficial bacteria are preserved. Pathogenic bacteria cannot survive in the salty, acidic brine and they die off. This fermentation process can be used to pickle just about any vegetable and many fruits.

The fermentation of sauerkraut is slightly different. Instead of pouring a salty brine over your sliced cabbage, massaging salt into the cabbage mixture serves to pull water from the cabbage cells, creating a brine in which the cabbage ferments. Just vegetables and salt. No heat is involved.

Both brine pickling and the fermentation of sauerkraut are forms of *lactic acid fermentation,* because the foods are preserved in an acidic medium—the lactic acid that is naturally generated by the lactic acid bacteria.

In other fermentation books, you'll see that some recipes call for whey, a fermentation starter, or brine from a previous batch of sauerkraut, thinking that the additional bacteria these starters provide are necessary for fermentation. However, the additional bacteria can interfere with the natural unfolding of the fermentation stages, and they are unnecessary, since the vegetables you're fermenting come with the bacteria necessary for fermentation. Therefore, none of my recipes call for starters.

Cultured is another term used in reference to fermented foods. I like to reserve this term for foods in which the addition of a culture is required to initiate the fermentation process, since natural bacteria are not present on some foods—yogurt, kombucha, or sourdough bread, for example.

To make yogurt, a dollop of yogurt (containing necessary bacteria from a previous batch) is mixed into warmed milk and left to culture for 8 to 24 hours in a warm place. During this time, the bacteria present in the yogurt go to work for us, growing and multiplying, to turn the milk into a thick, creamy product with a soured tang—more yogurt.

To make kombucha, a popular health drink, sweetened tea is mixed with a culture (kombucha from a previous batch of the fermented tea) and a SCOBY (a **s**ymbiotic **c**ulture **o**f **b**acteria and **y**east that grows in the fermenting tea). This is fermented for a week to produce an effervescent drink that helps the digestive system and detoxifies the body.

To make sourdough bread, flour and water are stirred together and left out in the kitchen to capture organisms in the environment. This creates a *starter culture* that causes the dough to rise and contributes marvelously complex, sour flavors to the finished product.

MEET YOUR NEIGHBORS

Fermentation is made possible by microscopic little beings found in our air, in the soil, and clinging to the vegetables grown in that soil. These are neighbors you never knew you had. Given the right conditions, these bacteria convert the sugars and carbohydrates in the vegetables into acids, carbon dioxide, and a very small amount of alcohol. These substances, in turn, preserve the food and add rich and complex flavors.

Whether the fermentation process is transforming a simple head of cabbage and humble vegetables into sauerkraut, milk into yogurt, tea into kombucha, or flour into bread, all it requires is the assistance of our microscopic neighbors, those wondrous microbes.

So, though I will do my best to teach you how best to harness the power of this microbial world, realize that you can't control it completely and have each jar of sauerkraut turn out the same. Each batch is different, and a batch made and fermented in my home may turn out slightly different from a batch made and fermented in your home, even if we use the exact same ingredients. This is because the mix of bacteria, yeasts, and other microbes hanging out in my kitchen and on my hands will most likely be different from the microbes in your kitchen and on your hands. And what you ferment in November will turn out differently than what you ferment in July.

FERMENTATION IS SAFE

Please trust in this centuries-old process. It is truly mind-boggling how simple and how safe fermentation is. Here are some words of comfort from a research microbiologist with the US Department of Agriculture who specializes in the safety of fermented and acidic foods:

> Risky *is not a word I would use to describe vegetable fermentation. It is one of the oldest and safest technologies we have... With fermented products there is no safety concern. I can flat-out say that. The reason is the lactic acid bacteria that carry out the fermentation are the world's best killers of other bacteria.*
>
> —Fred Breidt, USDA microbiologist

You cannot get botulism (a type of food poisoning) and die from eating naturally fermented foods. This is because early on in the fermentation process, the pH (acidity) of lacto-fermented vegetables drops to a level in which it is impossible for the toxin that causes botulism to establish itself. In addition, lactic acid is inhospitable to pathogenic bacteria (bad bacteria), which also cannot survive in the salty brine of the fermentation environment.

CHAPTER 2

Why Ferment?

During a moment of overload as you begin to learn how to ferment sauerkraut, you may want to just grab a can of it off the grocery store shelf and be done with it. Yes, it would save you the time and hassle of figuring out this whole fermentation thing, having to gather the necessary supplies, and then slicing a head of cabbage, but by going the easy route, you would lose out on so much. And I'm not just referring to the health benefits of naturally fermented sauerkraut over the canned and heat-processed stuff.

Here are some of the side benefits of fermenting sauerkraut yourself.

First off, there is the confidence gained by learning this time-honored process of making your own food and preserving a head of cabbage to eat at a later date. Many a proud moment has been shared by my blog readers as they taste the very first jar of sauerkraut they fermented.

Then, as understanding deepens, there is the sudden realization that you are living with trillions of wondrous bacteria—bacteria that we can't live without, bacteria that we certainly cannot ferment without. You develop a caring and appreciative relationship with these bacteria; you want to make sure you're properly feeding them, and you even begin to talk to them.

And maybe, as time goes on, you connect with the rhythms of nature and begin to look forward to each fruit or vegetable as it comes into season. Early spring spells leeks, asparagus, and beets. Early summer spells cucumbers, garlic, and carrots. Late summer spells corn, peppers, and cabbage. All these colorful vegetables can be fermented into some tasty pickle, relish, paste, or sauerkraut.

So, why is fermentation such a valuable process?

FERMENTATION PRESERVES YOUR FOOD

Through the ancient art of fermentation, starches and sugars in vegetables and fruits are converted into lactic acid by the many species of lactic-acid-producing bacteria, hence the often-used name *lacto-fermentation*. These bacteria are ubiquitous, present on the surface of all living things, and especially numerous on leaves and roots of plants growing in or near the ground. Lactic acid is a natural preservative that, during the process of fermentation, reduces pH to a level at which harmful bacteria cannot survive, retaining nutrients in the foods being fermented to prevent their spoilage.

It is by lactic acid that many fermented foods are *safely* preserved. This acidic fermentation renders foods resistant to spoilage and highly unlikely to develop food toxins.

This ancient practice has allowed cultures around the world to preserve and store food from the time of harvest to the time of consumption long before there were refrigerators, freezers, or canning.

FERMENTATION CUTS THE SUGAR CONTENT OF FOODS

During fermentation, the bacteria use the sugar present in the chopped vegetables as fuel for their work. As the bacteria work, they dramatically lower the sugar content of the foods being fermented.

During the fermentation of kombucha, the bacteria and yeasts in the added culture eat the sugars in the sweetened tea and produce a slightly sour drink. During the fermentation of sauerkraut, the sugars present in the cabbage are consumed by the bacteria, and the result is sauerkraut with a sour tang.

For wines and hard ciders, yeast present on the fruit helps to ferment sugars into alcohols.

FERMENTATION MAKES FOODS TASTE INCREDIBLE

Fermentation is a process that creates an awe-inspiring shift in the flavors of the food being fermented. This ancient practice changes grapes into wine, barley seeds into beer, milk into a whole smorgasbord of cheeses, flour into

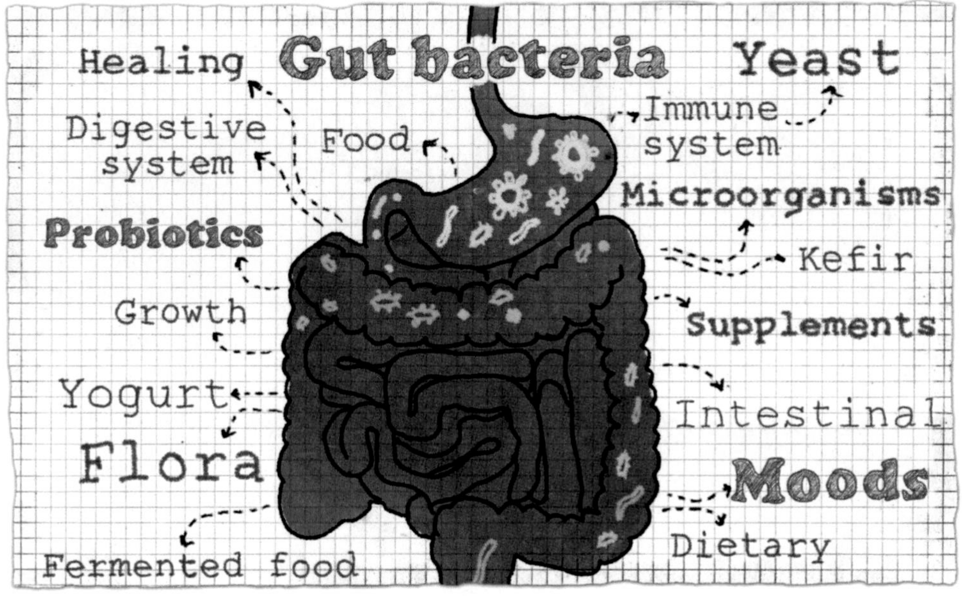

sourdough bread, soybeans into miso, cacao beans into chocolate, pork into prosciutto, cucumber into pickle, and cabbage into sauerkraut or kimchi. Now that you're salivating, need I say more?

Umami, which is Japanese for "pleasant savory taste," refers to glutamate—a type of amino acid that occurs naturally in many foods. When glutamate breaks down through fermentation, it becomes L-glutamate, and that's when things start to taste really good. The presence of L-glutamate is why properly fermented foods truly tantalize your taste buds.

FERMENTATION MAKES FOOD MORE DIGESTIBLE

Fermentation breaks down the nutrients and plant cells in foods into more digestible forms. Think of it as cooking without using heat. By using fermentation to "predigest" your foods, you greatly reduce the amount of work your digestive system has to do. Traditional cultures fermented not only vegetables but also grains, dairy, seeds, nuts, and meats.

All grains contain phytic acid, a natural compound that protects the grain's nutrients from being absorbed. Nature is trying to keep the grain intact so it can pass through any host undigested. Fermenting grains by soaking them before cooking neutralizes phytic acid, thereby rendering the grain far more nutritious. This is why sourdough bread made with a traditional starter and left to rise for 12–24 hours is far more nutritious and easier to digest than bread made with commercial brewer's yeast and a short rising time.

The fermentation process for producing fermented dairy products such as yogurt, kefir, and cultured butter converts the milk sugar known as lactose into lactic acid and breaks down the milk proteins, like casein, allowing for easier digestion.

FERMENTATION CREATES PROBIOTICS

Whereas *anti*biotics destroy microorganisms, *pro*biotics help to restore beneficial organisms in your digestive system. These live bacteria already exist on the vegetables you are fermenting, in the soil they were grown in, on your hands, and in the air. By setting up the right environment, you enable these bacteria—the *pro*biotics—to increase dramatically in numbers and diversity, thus providing you with an inexpensive source of beneficial organisms in your digestive system.

In one research study carried out for *Applied and Environmental Microbiology* on four different commercial fermentations, 686 types of bacteria were collected on days 1, 3, 7, and 14 of the fermentation process.[1] Researchers discovered that the species of lactic acid bacteria present in sauerkraut fermentations are more diverse than previously reported and varied greatly throughout the fermentation process.

FERMENTATION ENHANCES BIOAVAILABILITY

Bioavailability is the degree to which food nutrients are available for absorption and utilization in the body. Fermentation opens up cell walls in the cabbage to allow more vitamins and nutrients to be accessed and better absorbed by us humans. In addition, the digestive action of the bacteria not only increases the levels of existing nutrients, but in many cases generates additional nutrients as by-products of their metabolism.

FERMENTATION INCREASES ANTIOXIDANT POTENTIAL

When you ferment cabbage into sauerkraut, its vitamin C and antioxidant levels increase drastically. An antioxidant is a molecule that inhibits oxidation; oxidation is a chemical reaction that leads to chain reactions that damage cells by producing free radicals. Antioxidants, such as ascorbic acid (vitamin C) in fruit, betanin in beets, and glucosinolate in cabbage, protect us against chronic diseases.

Raw cabbage contains moderate amounts of vitamin C, around 30 milligrams per cup. Levels of vitamin C in a cup of sauerkraut range from 57 to 695 milligrams per cup, with raw, fermented red cabbage having the highest levels of vitamin C, hitting almost 700 milligrams per cup.[2]

SAUERKRAUT FUN FACT

In the eighteenth century, explorers like Captain Cook used sauerkraut to prevent scurvy during long sea voyages, bringing as much as 25,000 pounds of the vitamin C–rich ferment along on voyages.

FERMENTATION REMOVES TOXINS

During fermentation, pesticide residues and other toxins present on what is being fermented are broken down and degraded.

A 2009 study by Gyeongsang National University in Korea examined the role of microorganisms in the degradation of insecticides during the fermentation of kimchi.[3] At the onset of fermentation, the kimchi was inoculated with the insecticide chlorpyrifos (CP). The CP degraded rapidly until day 3 and degraded completely by day 9. Four different lactic-acid-producing bacterial strains (*Leuconostoc mesenteroides, Lactobacillus brevis, Lactobacillus plantarum*, and *Lactobacillus sakei*) were identified as the responsible bacteria. There's no need for you to memorize these names, though *Lactobacillus plantarum* is the one you'll often see listed on probiotic supplement jars and cited when identifying which bacteria have the most beneficial health effects.

A 2008 study done by the Iranian Agricultural Engineering Research Institute examined the potential of isolated lactic acid bacteria in the degradation of agricultural pesticide residue (malathion and diazinon) during the fermentation process.[4] The initial concentrations of malathion and diazinon in the vegetable (unprocessed sample) were 3.5 and 0.6 milligrams per kilogram respectively. After 48 hours of fermentation, the concentration of malathion considerably decreased and reached 0.5 milligrams per kilogram, whereas diazinon concentration only decreased about 0.1 milligrams per kilogram. The remarkable degradation of the malathion during fermentation could be attributed to its instability at low pH ranges.

FERMENTATION INEXPENSIVELY CREATES NUTRIENTS

Fermentation is a simple, budget-friendly process that provides an inexpensive way to get a wide range of nutrients. All you need is a repurposed canning jar, a head of cabbage, and some salt. Then, with the help of some bacteria and a bit of time, you have lactic acid that activates enzymes in your colon for improved digestion; gut-healing probiotics; the multi-vitamin potential of increased vitamins, minerals, and extra nutrients through bioavailability; and more vitamin C and other antioxidants than you started with. All for the cost of a head of cabbage.

CHAPTER 3

How Fermented Foods Supercharge Health

Fermented foods are made either by using a culture to inoculate food or allowing ingredients to ferment over time in a controlled environment, often adding salt to draw moisture out of the food and keep bad bacteria at bay while the good bacteria multiply and grow, enhancing the nutritional profile of the ingredients.

This fermentation process converts the sugars into cellular energy, with lactic acid being its byproduct. It's this lactic acid that then produces digestive enzymes and healthy gut flora, and cuts the sugar content of the food at the same time! The result is good-for-you foods full of vitamins, minerals, enzymes, and probiotics.

Probiotics attack pathogenic bacteria and strengthen your good bacteria, which sets you up to be more resistant to future invasions of pathogens. It's important to note that most probiotics are transient bacteria, which means they will only last a few days in the body, so it's a good idea to regularly consume probiotic-rich foods.

You'll also want to consume foods rich in prebiotics to feed these important inhabitants of your gut microbiome. Prebiotics are food-borne fuel for the beneficial bacteria that live in the gut, and they occur in raw garlic, cooked and raw onions, leeks, chicory, Jerusalem artichokes, jicama, and other fiber-rich foods.

Here is a list of benefits derived from consuming fermented foods.

FERMENTED FOODS FLAVORFULLY DELIVER NUMEROUS NUTRIENTS AND PROBIOTICS

Sauerkraut is a good source of fiber, antioxidants, and living enzymes and is rich in vitamins and minerals, along with beneficial probiotics, all critical for optimal health. Probiotics are the bacteria present on the vegetables, fermented and grown during fermentation. These various strains of probiotics help make foods more digestible and increase your gut's ability to absorb nutrients.

Here is a list of the approximate nutrients and percent daily value (DV)* in two heaping forkfuls of sauerkraut, which is a 2-ounce (57 g) serving, a good daily dose:[5]

- 20 calories
- 0 grams fat
- 2 grams fiber
- 4 grams carbohydrates
- 2 grams sugar
- 1 grams protein
- 480 milligrams sodium, 14% DV
- 100 milligrams potassium, 3% DV
- 75 milligrams vitamin C, 30% DV
- 10 milligrams vitamin K, 45% DV
- 40 milligrams calcium, 2% DV
- 1 milligrams iron, 6% DV
- 17 micrograms folate, 6% DV

*Percent daily values are based on a 2,000 calorie diet.

But the main reason many of us consume sauerkraut is for the probiotics. *Lactobacillus plantarum* and *Lactobacillus acidophilus* are a couple of the superstars found in sauerkraut.

Lactobacillus plantarum is extremely hardy and survives the acidic conditions of the stomach as it makes its way to your colon to colonize your gut. *Lactobacillus plantarum* is known for its ability to create the hydrogen peroxide that your body uses as a defence against pathogenic bacteria, as well as bacteria consumed in foods.

Lactobacillus acidophilus colonizes most densely in the small intestine, where it helps maintain the integrity of the intestinal wall, ensures proper nutrient absorption, and supports healthy overall digestive function.

FERMENTED FOODS MAXIMIZE THE HEALTH OF YOUR GUT MICROBIOME

Two thousand years ago Hippocrates, the father of modern medicine, said, "All disease begins in the gut." This quote has been proven even more valuable as we begin to better understand the importance of including probiotic-rich foods in our diet. What we eat impacts the different gut bacteria residing in our digestive tracts, as well as the integrity of the gut lining.

Your body is home to trillions of microscopic visitors that make up your unique microbiome fingerprint. Each of us harbors a personal set of microbes that, like our fingerprints, has the potential to uniquely identify us. This troop of bacterial superheroes living in your gut work very hard to help keep you healthy, strong, and resilient. They extract energy from the foods you eat and act as sentinels for your immune system. They are in constant communication with your brain and the rest of your body, sending and receiving messages to control your hormones, your appetite, and your preferred foods, among other functions. Your existence depends on these microbes, and their existence depends on you. Feed them well and they will protect you.

FERMENTED FOODS SUPPORT YOUR IMMUNE SYSTEM

Most people, and many physicians, do not realize that 70–80% of the cells that make up your immune system are found in the walls of your gut. The consumption of fermented foods supports the health of the gut lining (mucosa) as a natural barrier. A lack of beneficial bacteria allows disease-causing microbes to take hold in your gut, causing inflammation in the gut wall, or even slip through a weakened gut wall and run rampant in the rest of the body.

FERMENTED FOODS PROMOTE GOOD DIGESTIVE HEALTH

By eating a variety of fermented foods, you supply your digestive tract with a wide range of beneficial bacteria that help promote the growth of healthy flora in your intestines. This makes for better digestion, which makes for better health.

Having a healthy balance of gut flora and plenty of digestive enzymes ensures that you will absorb more of the nutrients in the foods you eat. When your gut flora is out of balance, you can't absorb all the nutrients out of the foods you eat.

In addition, eating sauerkraut can compensate for decreased production of hydrochloric acid, our stomach's natural secretion that decreases as we age. Hydrochloric acid acts as a barrier to prevent harmful bacteria and parasites from invading your digestive system. Hydrochloric acid also improves digestion in your stomach by breaking down food so it can be absorbed by the small intestine. The lactic acid from sauerkraut can partially compensate for reduced hydrochloric acid.

Your pancreas produces a variety of essential digestive enzymes that break down starches, proteins, and fats. Unpasteurized sauerkraut is high in viable enzymes that work just like the ones from the pancreas.

FERMENTED FOODS POTENTIALLY LOWER YOUR CHOLESTEROL

Fermented foods have been shown to decrease heart disease risk by lowering LDL (bad) cholesterol levels and raising HDL (good) cholesterol. Kimchi—and sauerkraut—contains bioactive compounds that lower cholesterol by blocking cholesterol from being absorbed into the bloodstream.[6] *Lactobacillus plantarum* has also been shown to help lower cholesterol.[7]

FERMENTED FOODS REDUCE YOUR CHANCES OF CONTRACTING FOODBORNE ILLNESSES

Have you ever wondered why not everyone who ate the latest round of contaminated spinach got sick? Over one million Americans suffer from foodborne illnesses annually, but you don't have to be one of them. Foodborne illnesses are often caused by pathogenic bacteria. By strengthening your immune system, you are far less likely to be struck with diarrhea, nausea, vomiting, or any of the other gnarly symptoms from consuming contaminated food.

This is because fermented foods are rich in probiotics that help create a protective lining in the intestines, making it difficult for illness-causing pathogenic bacteria, such as salmonella and E. coli, to take hold.

FERMENTED FOODS LESSEN YOUR RISKS FOR CERTAIN CANCERS

Eating sauerkraut may reduce incidence of breast cancer. Researchers fed mice a fast-food diet. Compared to controls, these mice had a predisposition to breast cancer. Researchers then repeated these trials but gave some of these fast-food mice the probiotic *Lactobacillus reuteri*. Those mice that received the probiotic had a significantly lower rate of breast cancer symptoms than those that didn't.

Cabbage and other cruciferous vegetables, such as bok choy, brussels sprouts, turnips, radish, and cauliflower, are rich sources of glucosinolate. During fermentation, glucosinolate breaks down into different compounds known as isothiocyanates, a class of antioxidants that has been shown in laboratory studies to prevent the growth of cancer.

The researchers go on to suggest that *Lactobacillus reuteri* may be increasing the development of a certain type of immune cell that may be responsible for exerting the underlying anticancer effects they are observing.[8]

FERMENTED FOODS BOOST YOUR MOOD AND REVITALIZE YOUR MIND

Your brain's health, and how you feel both mentally and physically, is dictated by the state of your gut microbiome. Think of the last time you felt sick to your stomach because you were anxious or scared. Just as your brain can send butterflies to your stomach, your gut can relay a state of calm to your brain. The relationship between the gut and the brain is bidirectional.

The vagus nerve, the longest of the 12 cranial nerves, is the primary channel between the millions of nerve cells in our enteric nervous system (the nervous system embedded in the lining of the intestinal tract) and our central nervous system (the brain and spinal cord). In fact, there are more neurons in your enteric nervous system than there are in your central nervous system, leading many scientists to call the gut the "second brain." Your gut's brain makes more serotonin—the master happiness molecule—than the brain in your head. In addition, GABA, an amino acid produced by gut bacteria, calms nerve activity. And glutamate, a neurotransmitter produced by gut bacteria, is involved in cognition, learning, and memory.

FERMENTED FOODS HELP YOU LOSE WEIGHT

The extra weight you might carry can be caused by an imbalance in your gut microbiome. There are millions of bacteria living in your gut. While a majority of them are good, destructive bacteria that crave all the wrong foods live there too. These bad bacteria alter the way you process and hold onto fat, and send messages to your brain to feed them even when you are not hungry.

What you eat is hugely important when it comes to balancing your gut microbiome. When you feast on sugar and processed foods, you're encouraging the growth of the bad bacteria. When you add fermented foods—like sauerkraut—to your diet, you encourage the growth of the good bacteria. In addition, consuming foods rich in prebiotics will feed your good bacteria to help them repopulate your gut and starve your bad bacteria so you can improve your digestion and shrink your waistline.

SAUERKRAUT FUN FACT

Sauerkraut is a time-honored folk remedy for canker sores. It is used by rinsing the mouth with sauerkraut juice for about 30 seconds several times a day, or by placing a wad of sauerkraut against the affected area for a minute or so before chewing and swallowing the kraut.

CHAPTER 4

Why to Make Sauerkraut Your One Ferment

Why a whole book devoted to sauerkraut? Because learning to make sauerkraut is an inexpensive way to learn to ferment, the knowledge and skills you learn can be applied to your next fermentation endeavor, and it's easy to include this probiotic-rich ferment in your diet.

SAUERKRAUT FUN FACT

The word *sauerkraut* is from the German *Sauerkraut*, which literally means "sour cabbage": *sauer* (sour) + *kraut* (vegetable, cabbage).

SAUERKRAUT: THE GATEWAY DRUG OF FERMENTATION

If this is your first foray into fermentation, you may soon discover just why it's often said in fermentation circles that sauerkraut is the "gateway drug" of fermentation. Why?

- The entry fee is low and the barriers are minimal.
- It's simple to make.
- No fancy jars are required.
- There's no need to purchase expensive equipment.
- It can be made with a variety of flavoring ingredients to make it extra delicious.
- It's a ferment that pairs well with just about anything, making it a dead simple way to take advantage of its probiotic benefits.
- It keeps well, and you will save oodles of money over buying that expensive designer sauerkraut you find in natural food stores.
- It's a habit-forming skill that will lead you to the discovery of other foods to ferment.
- And it's delicious.

Just cabbage, salt, time, and ... some freeloading bacteria, which you'll learn about in part 2.

SAUERKRAUT: THE ONE THING

Make sauerkraut your gateway drug of choice, the one thing to learn how to ferment. Then enjoy adding this one thing to your meals to make significant changes to your health and well-being with minimal effort. Just a forkful of this one thing contains billions of beneficial microbes that nourish and repair your gut!

SAUERKRAUT FUN FACT

The Germans gave sauerkraut its popular name, but they did not invent it. Sauerkraut originated nearly 2,000 years ago in ancient China. In summer, slaves building the Great Wall of China lived on cabbage and rice. In winter, the cabbage was preserved with rice wine, which soured the cabbage, to keep thousands of laborers healthy in the worst of conditions.

MINIMUM EFFECTIVE DOSE

> *When I first began eating sauerkraut, I noticed a significant difference in how I felt within four days. After one week, evening belly bloat disappeared, recurring constipation was gone, and I felt more energetic and just plain healthy!*
>
> —Cindy

These results are helpful to know if you're trying to get used to the idea of eating something that's been left to rot on your counter for weeks! You don't have to eat much of it to get results; just a forkful will do.

Tim Ferriss, author of *The 4-Hour Workweek, The 4-Hour Body,* and *The 4-Hour Chef,* tailors much of his work, exercise, and cooking around what he calls the "minimum effective dose" (MED). MED is simply the minimum effective dose that will produce the desired outcome. The idea is that you can make significant changes in your life with minimal effort.

I first got into making fermented foods, soaking grains and nuts, sourcing and culturing raw dairy, and preparing grass-fed meat to improve my health. However, the number of hours I was spending in the kitchen was driving me crazy, resulting in high-stress levels. Not so good for my health. I had to do something about it. What do I cut out? What do I focus on?

I took Tim Ferriss's MED to heart and made a daily forkful of sauerkraut, my MED of healthy foods. Yes, I still tried to properly source and prepare the other foods my family ate, but by keeping my refrigerator stocked with sauerkraut and letting some of the other healthy food ideas go, I soon was able to get the nourishment I needed without the stress.

The trillions of beneficial bacteria in that little bit of sauerkraut was my MED for improved health. They kept my digestion moving along smoothly, my energy humming, and my immune system strong.

Always have a jar handy. Place a dollop on your plate. Savor!

PART 2

Getting Started

In this section I will set the foundation for successful fermentation by opening chapter 5 with three key concepts: get the salt right, keep your ferment under the brine, and learn first by fermenting in small batches. Grasp these concepts and confidence grows, skills skyrocket, and fermentation success is almost guaranteed.

In chapter 6 (p.25), we cover three essential ingredients for making sauerkraut: cabbage, salt, and a secret ingredient. There are tips to help you choose the best cabbage, the best salt—and how much of it—along with a critical ingredient that is seldom, if ever, listed in a recipe. Get to know that ingredient, understand how to take care of it, treat it well, and you will be fermenting mouthwatering sauerkraut.

In chapter 7 (p.31), I detail what you need for your first batch of sauerkraut, most of which you probably already own. I packed my first batch of sauerkraut into a 1-quart (1 L) canning jar I had around the house, weighted down with some decorative glass gems—the kind used in floral arrangements—and sealed with a standard canning lid and ring. It was a place to start. It worked. As your understanding of fermentation evolves, the tools you use will grow along with you, so you'll want to return time and time again to this chapter. Let's get started.

CHAPTER 5

Three Key Concepts to Help You Master This Ancient Art of Preservation

Fermentation is an ancient method of preservation that has been used reliably for thousands of years. However, since most of us did not grow up learning this art, it can seem intimidating and not sound very safe. If one is accustomed to buying vegetables sealed in cans and jars that have been processed at high temperatures, it becomes counterintuitive to let fresh food sit out on our counter for days, if not weeks.

However, by understanding just a few key concepts, you can turn from fearing bacteria to welcoming them into your world and making their home as comfortable for them as possible.

KEY CONCEPT #1: SALT IS NECESSARY FOR FERMENTATION

All fruits and vegetables harbor large and diverse populations of bacteria, some good and some not so good. When we use these vegetables for fermentation, we are orchestrating a competition, a microbial race, so to speak, between the pathogenic or "bad" bacteria—along with molds and yeasts—and the beneficial or "good" bacteria on these vegetables and in the environment. Salt is your key weapon to ensure that the good guys win the race.

SALT MAKES FERMENTATION SAFE

Salt ensures that the good guys can grow and proliferate to win the microbial race of fermentation. In chapter 6, I'll describe the various salts on the market in detail. For now, know that salt is essential for safe fermentation.

When you mix salt into a bowl of shredded cabbage, almost immediately you'll notice it start to glisten. Through the process of osmosis, salt extracts water from the cells in the vegetables to create a brine that the cabbage mixture is then packed in. In this brine, the good guys (the salt-tolerant bacteria) grow, thrive, and convert sugars naturally present in vegetables into lactic acid. This lactic acid then lowers the pH of your ferment to create an environment in which the salt-phobic pathogenic bacteria cannot live.

SALT GIVES A LOVELY CRISPY CRUNCH TO YOUR SAUERKRAUT

Salt hardens the plant cell compounds called pectin in your vegetables and slows down the action of the pectin-digesting enzymes (pectinase), enhancing their flavors and texture. Without salt, cabbage would turn to mush, rot, and fall apart.

SALT ENABLES THE SALT-TOLERANT BACTERIA TO CREATE THE PRESERVATIVE FOR YOUR SAUERKRAUT

Salt enables your vegetables to properly ferment and create lactic acid. Lactic acid is a natural preservative. Salt also slows down fermentation, slows down the pectin-digesting bacteria, and prevents the development of surface mold, to preserve your sauerkraut.

SALT ACTS AS A FLAVOR ENHANCER

Salt acts to reduce bitterness, and at the concentration used in fermentation, it suppresses sweetness and enhances *umami,* or savory taste. *Umami,* which is Japanese for "pleasant savory taste," refers to glutamate—a type of amino acid that occurs naturally in many foods. When glutamate breaks down through fermentation, it becomes L-glutamate, and that's when things start to taste really good. The presence of L-glutamate is why properly fermented foods truly tantalize your taste buds.

I'M ON A SALT-RESTRICTED DIET. CAN I FERMENT WITHOUT SALT?

No! Recipes that substitute ingredients high in naturally occurring sodium—such as celery juice, seaweeds, or specific herbs—for salt risk creating a brine at a salinity outside the recommended range for safe fermentation. Adding a packaged starter culture, as many no-salt fermentation recipes call for, does not alter the salinity.

Remember, when sauerkraut is consumed as a condiment—just a forkful or two—you're still consuming vast amounts of beneficial bacteria and just a modest amount of sodium. One 30-gram (1 oz) serving of sauerkraut—one heaping forkful—contains 243 milligrams of sodium.

KEY CONCEPT #2: VEGETABLE FERMENTATION IS AN ANAEROBIC PROCESS

One of the key factors in the successful fermentation of sauerkraut and other vegetables is keeping your ferment below the brine. When vegetables are submerged under the brine, the lactic acid bacteria (LAB) responsible for fermentation—which are *anaerobic*—are able to grow and thrive. LAB do not require oxygen. In contrast, *aerobic* bacteria, some being pathogenic—*Salmonella* and *E. coli,* for example—require an oxygen-rich environment.

From the moment your vegetables are harvested, they begin to decay. Microorganisms in the environment—both the good guys and the bad guys—begin to feed on the moisture and nutrients in the cabbage. If left to their own devices in a warm spot on your kitchen counter, the *aerobic* bacteria would turn your cabbage into a smelly, rotten mass.

If, instead, you mix just the right amount of salt in with that cabbage to create a brine, pack that wet cabbage mixture into a jar, and then hold it below the brine with a weight, you will have created the perfect home for a totally different set of bacteria. These are the *anaerobic* bacteria (the ones that function without oxygen), mainly *Leuconostoc mesenteroides, Lactobacillus plantarum,* and *Lactobacillus pentoaceticus.* In this environment, these good guys will then grow, proliferate, and make lactic acid, creating an acidic environment that will kill off the pathogenic bacteria, and in the process perfectly preserve your cabbage.

KEY CONCEPT #3: THE JAR IS YOUR TEACHER

Please, please, please do not let your newfound enthusiasm for fermentation get the better of you. Do not make your first batch of sauerkraut in a large stoneware crock, even if you were just gifted a beautiful crock or recently unearthed your grandmother's prized pickle crock. Instead choose a 1-quart (1 L) glass canning jar for fermenting your first few batches of sauerkraut.

Glass canning jars make fermentation a very doable task, allowing for quick successes and immediate feedback. You'll quickly know the following:

If you're using the right amount of salt. Fermentation best unfolds with a set amount of salt, but there is a slight bit of wiggle room in the numbers. If your first batch tastes way too salty, you'll know to use a bit less in subsequent batches or switch to a different salt.

If you are keeping your ferment anaerobic. Usually, with the correct amount of salt, a proper weight, and the right lid, your ferment stays submerged below the brine, little or no air gets into your jar, and no mold grows. However, if you are one of the unfortunate few and mold invades your jar, you can figure out what caused it and make alterations for the next batch.

Observe and understand the normal stages of fermentation. Bubbles rising to the surface? All that brine? Things seeming suddenly quiet? Have the bacteria gone on strike? Colors shifting from bright green to pale yellow? A rather strong odor permeating your household that some love and some find offensive? With a clear jar, you can observe these changes, learn what is causing them, and also watch in awe as the bacteria transform salty cabbage to sour sauerkraut.

What flavors of sauerkraut you and your family prefer. Sauerkraut has an unfamiliar tang and taste for most of us when eating it for the first time. By experimenting with various recipes, you'll discover the flavors that you or your family truly enjoy.

And best of all? Fermenting in glass jars builds confidence. Confidence to make larger batches of sauerkraut in a crock if desired, or to branch out and try other types of fermenting. Sour kefir? Bubbly kombucha? Flavorful relishes? Garlic paste? Natural pickles? The confidence and skills you develop from fermenting in a jar will guide you on your exploration of the beautiful, big world of fermentation.

CHAPTER 6

Three Essential Ingredients

Bacteria, salt, and cabbage are the three essential ingredients to always carry in your fermentation toolbox if you're to successfully ferment countless batches of sauerkraut. When this rather simple set of ingredients is combined in just the right ratios and properly packed into a suitable container, a wondrous alchemy unfolds. And with time, your salty cabbage is transformed into sour sauerkraut.

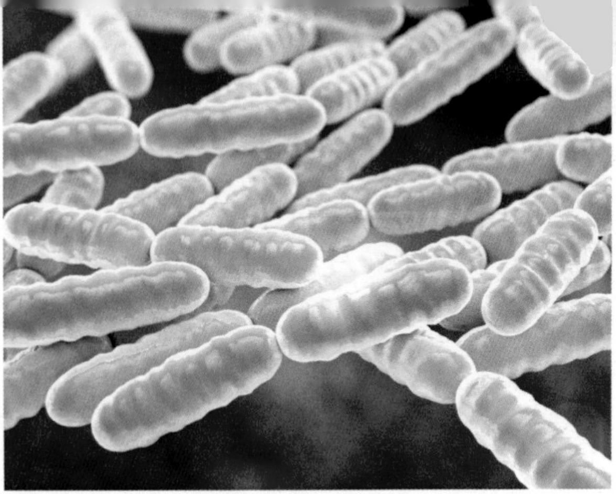

1. BACTERIA: INVISIBLE BUT CRUCIAL WORKER BEES IN YOUR FERMENT

Not only would we not exist if it weren't for bacteria, but a vast set of mouthwatering fermented foods would not be possible without bacteria. Don't worry, there is no need to go shopping for these bacteria. The lactic acid bacteria necessary for fermentation hitch a free ride on the produce you ferment. They are present on the surface of all living things and especially numerous on the leaves and roots of plants growing in or near the ground, such as cabbage!

These bacteria eat the sugars in cabbage and produce lactic acid, which then lowers the pH to create an acidic environment which preserves your sauerkraut, inhibits the formation and growth of putrefying bacteria, and gives sauerkraut its tangy flavor.

If you were to purchase bacteria, you would buy a *fermentation starter,* or a rather expensive packet of bacteria. These starters contain several strains of bacteria, along with fillers, sugars, and other ingredients you might not want in your sauerkraut, and may interfere with the natural progression of the stages of fermentation.

2. SALT: CREATOR OF THE BRINE IN WHICH FERMENTATION TAKES PLACE

Salt plays a central role in the fermentation process. Salt pulls water out of the cabbage cells to create a salty brine in which good bacteria can thrive and grow and bad bacteria die off. Without salt, a bowl of sliced cabbage left to sit on the counter for days, if not weeks, really would become a rotten, smelly, putrefying mess.

Salt comes in all colors (pink, red, blue, green, grey, and black), shapes, and sizes, from all corners of the globe. All salts originate from a sea or salty body of water. Some salts come from dried lake beds, some from mined deposits of seawater that crystallized more than 200 million years ago, and some from salt water that has been dried by wind and sun.

At its core, salt (NaCl) is a crystalline mineral made of two elements, sodium (Na) and chlorine (Cl), which are essential not only for human health but for the health of the bacteria in your ferment. Many salts contain iodine, an essential micronutrient that was first added to salt in 1924 to maintain thyroid gland health. However, since iodine's antibacterial properties can interfere with the fermentation process, it is best to use an iodine-free salt for fermentation.

WHICH SALT SHOULD I USE?

The best salt for fermentation is a mineral-rich salt. These types of salt still have their complete natural profile of minerals, to add not only a depth of flavor to your ferment but additional food for the bacteria. One of the nutritional benefits of fermentation is that it makes minerals bioavailable, resulting in a more nutritious sauerkraut. So, the more minerals there are in the salt you use, the more minerals you'll end up with in your sauerkraut. Himalayan pink salt and Redmond Real Salt are both commonly found mineral-rich salts.

BEST	OKAY	NOT RECOMMENDED
Himalayan pink salt Redmond Real Salt	Sea salt Pickling salt	Table salt Iodized salt Kosher salt Grey sea salts

BEST

HIMALAYAN PINK SEA SALT (FINE GRAIN)—MY FAVORITE

Himalayan pink salt is mined from deposits from ancient geological oceans deep under the Himalayan mountains and contains more than 84 trace minerals, including potassium, calcium, magnesium, iodine, iron, and zinc. Its pink color comes from trace amounts of iron oxide (rust) that is found naturally in the salt. This salt crystallized more than 200 million years ago and remains protected from modern-day pollution and impurities.

When selecting a Himalayan pink salt, make sure it comes from Pakistan, the only true source of real Himalayan salt. Expect to pay about $3.50 to $5.00 per pound. Prices much lower than this may be a sign that the salt was collected from higher elevations, rather than the deeper, more pure salt mines, and may contain impurities—impurities that you may notice settling to the bottom of your container when dissolving some salt in water to make a brine.

To ensure that your salt easily dissolves, ideally purchase fine-grain salt. If all you are able to get is a coarse salt sold in a grinder, grind it before measuring.

REDMOND REAL SALT—ALSO A GREAT CHOICE

Redmond Real Salt comes from an ancient sea bed in central Utah. It is a completely natural sea salt—with more than 60 trace minerals and not chemically treated or bleached.

Redmond Real Salt is commonly found in health food stores and even in many standard grocery stores. Some notice a harmless sandy residue when dissolving Redmond Real Salt in water. If this is a concern, select a high-quality Himalayan pink salt.

SEA SALT—CHECK THE LABEL

Sea salt comes from evaporating seawater. Most so-called sea salt is produced by industrial methods, is highly refined, and has had all its minerals stripped out during processing, just like table salt. As long as there are no additives listed on the label, it will work just fine.

PICKLING SALT—WORKS FINE

Pickling salt does not contain anti-caking ingredients or additives like iodine. Pickling salt is pure granulated salt (sodium chloride). In addition, its fine granules are easily dissolved.

NOT RECOMMENDED

KOSHER SALT—NOT RECOMMENDED

This is also a popular salt found in most grocery stores. Kosher salt is not kosher itself, but is used to make meats kosher and has a larger crystal than table salt; this larger crystal means it doesn't dissolve as rapidly as a fine-grain salt, and this slowing down of the solution is not desirable.

It is less likely to contain additives like anti-caking agents and iodine, but check the label and then take a bit more time when creating your brine to make sure the larger salt crystals are completely dissolved.

CELTIC SEA SALT, GREY SEA SALT, AND FRENCH GREY SEA SALT—NOT RECOMMENDED

These salts contain naturally occurring minerals, have a high moisture content, and can contain dirt, especially with salts that are grey or brown. Some contain high levels of lead and other heavy metals, due to the high levels of pollution in our waters today. In addition, their actual sodium content depends on the drying method and varies greatly from company to company.

TABLE SALT OR IODIZED SALT—DO NOT USE

These are basic, widely-used salts that you can buy inexpensively from any grocery store. They are refined salts that have had all their minerals stripped out during processing, with anti-caking agents added to prevent clumping, along with iodine to eliminate thyroid problems like goiter.

3. CABBAGE: THE FOUNDATION OF ANY SAUERKRAUT

Cabbage, the star player in the creation of sauerkraut, is a superfood beyond compare. All cruciferous vegetables in the cabbage family are anticancer foods. Cabbage is also a rich stimulant for digestive enzymes and will stimulate a healthy balance of stomach acid. In addition, cabbage is rich in sulforaphane, which supports the body's production of detoxification enzymes, and this has antioxidant effects.

SAUERKRAUT FUN FACT

Cabbage is a cruciferous vegetable belonging to the mustard family, *Brassicaceae*. You'll also find kohlrabi, kale, broccoli, brussels sprouts, and cauliflower in this family.

You can use any variety of cabbage in your sauerkraut: green, red, napa, or savoy. However, for your first few batches of sauerkraut, I recommend that you use standard green cabbage. It ferments fabulously, which is one more way to guarantee success, and it gives you a baseline to gauge how future batches are fermenting. The better your ingredients, the better the finished product will be. Ideally, only organic produce should be used when fermenting. Not only do vegetables sprayed with pesticides have many of the beneficial bacteria killed off, but they tend to have lower levels of the many nutrients that are food for the bacteria that will transform the vegetables you used into delicious probiotics. The greater the nutrition in the vegetables you are using, the more food the beneficial bacteria will have to eat, and the better they will work for you. Feed them well.

However, if organic cabbage is not accessible or affordable, here are a couple of things to keep in mind. One, cabbage sits toward the top of the Environmental Working Group's annual list of "Clean 15," or produce with the least likelihood to contain pesticide residue.[9]

Two, as noted under the benefits of fermentation, bacteria can significantly reduce pesticide residues in food.

So, if you are unable to obtain entirely chemical-free produce, appreciate the power of bacteria and recognize the value of fermenting foods.

GREEN CABBAGE

Green Cabbage is my favorite when it comes to making sauerkraut. This king of the cabbage world has wide fan-like leaves that are pale green in color and hold together well through the fermentation process. I almost always use the traditional round-headed green cabbage, because it is commonly grown by my local farmers, has a nice texture, and retains most of its crunch throughout the fermentation process.

SAUERKRAUT FUN FACT

The world's largest cabbage is credited to Scott Robb of Palmer, Alaska, whose record-setting giant cabbage weighed in at 138.25 pounds at the Alaska State Fair in 2013. Robb credits the massive growth to long summer days. "Since it really doesn't get dark during an Alaskan summer, the cabbage growth doesn't really shut down but continues to lumber along and grow."

RED CABBAGE

Red cabbage, though similar in shape to green cabbage, is a tad deeper and earthier in flavor, with tougher leaves. Its tougher leaves mean it will take longer to ferment than traditional green cabbage. In addition, red cabbage is rich in anthocyanins, the compound that gives red cabbage—and blueberries, Concord grapes, and black tomatoes—its distinctive dark color. Anthocyanins also act as antioxidants and are believed to have anti-inflammatory properties.

SAVOY CABBAGE

Savoy cabbage is a beautiful cabbage with textured leaves. It is shaped like green cabbage but with tender, deeply crinkled leaves that will ferment more quickly than common green cabbage.

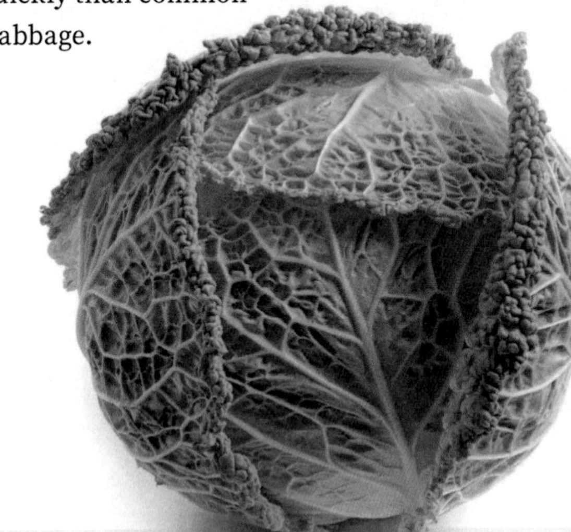

NAPA CABBAGE

Napa cabbage, also called Chinese cabbage, is an oblong-shaped cabbage that is milder and sweeter than green cabbage. It has white stalks and crinkly, light yellow to pale green leaves. Napa cabbage is traditionally grown all over Asia and is prized for its soft, fleshy, juicy leaves, which form the core of any kimchi recipe.

CABBAGE SELECTION GUIDE

Cabbage is available year-round in most markets, enabling you to make sauerkraut throughout the year. Specific varieties of cabbage fall into two broad categories: summer and winter.

Summer cabbage is sown in early spring and harvested throughout the summer. Summer cabbages grow faster and tend to have thinner leaves and an overall lower moisture content.

Winter cabbage is usually sown in late summer and harvested in late fall. Winter cabbages grow slower and have thicker leaves and a higher moisture content, making winter cabbage ideally suited for sauerkraut. Farmers usually wait until there have been a few light frosts to harvest winter cabbage. Cabbage reacts to cold conditions and frost by producing sugars, making it taste rather sweet.

When purchasing cabbage, select for size, sweetness, and freshness:

Size. Choose heads that seem heavy for their size, an indication of freshness. The tighter the cabbage leaves, the easier the head is to slice.

Sweetness. Sugar levels in your cabbage can vary quite a bit depending on variety and growing conditions. The sweeter the cabbage, the greater the depth of flavors obtained, and the better fermentation unfolds. Taste a few slices of the raw cabbage, staying away from heads that taste bitter.

Freshness. The fresher the cabbage, the more brine it will create. Most cabbage is grown in the fall, stored throughout the year, and shipped to the stores as requested. During storage, it dries out. This loss of moisture means the cabbage can create less brine. Cabbages that are light for their size, with outer leaves that are wilted, brown, or excessively torn, could be older. Check the bottom of the cabbage to be sure the leaves are not beginning to separate from the stem, an indication of age.

CHAPTER 7

The Basic Equipment for Your Fermentation Laboratory

START WITH THE BASICS AND WHAT IS READILY FOUND AROUND THE HOME. MAKE A FEW BATCHES AND THEN UPGRADE AS YOU SEE FIT.

DO I NEED TO STERILIZE MY EQUIPMENT?

It is certainly important to work with clean hands, utensils, and equipment, but sterile conditions are an unnecessary extra step. Simply wash jars, lids, and tools with soapy water and thoroughly rinse.

Sterilizing your equipment with bleach or other strong agents, or using vegetable rinses, may actually backfire. The lactic acid bacteria that are crucial for fermentation live on vegetables, on our hands, and in the air. Destroying every last one of them with strong agents or high heat leaves nothing behind to make fermentation happen. You want as much of the lactic acid bacteria as possible to beat out the bad guys in the microbial race you will be organizing in your jar of fermenting sauerkraut.

FERMENTATION VESSEL: PROVIDE A SAFE HOME FOR THE BACTERIA

The first item to select when getting ready to ferment is the container you will be packing your sauerkraut mixture into. The best vessel to use when learning how to make sauerkraut is a glass jar.

CANNING JAR

A simple wide-mouth quart (liter) canning jar is the perfect fermentation vessel for beginners and pros alike. Canning jars

- are inexpensive to purchase or easy to find used,
- allow you to make fermentation a very doable task,
- are clear, which allows you to watch the fermentation process unfold,
- make it easy to experiment with various recipes or try unusual vegetable combinations,
- can be used both for fermentation and for storage, and
- fit easily into your refrigerator and can be served out of directly.

REPURPOSED JAR

If you live in an area of the world where canning jars are not easily purchased, repurpose jars that have been used for other food items. Ideally, find jars that are about the 1-quart (1 L) size and have a wide opening. Jars much smaller than this make it much harder to create a strong and healthy fermentation. It is also nice to stick to the same size jar in order for quantities to be kept consistent from batch to batch.

OTHER JARS

Fido-style jars with a bail top, clamp-down lidded jars, and jar-sized fermentation kits with specialty lids and/or weights all make great fermentation vessels.

SAUERKRAUT FUN FACT

In World War I and World War II, the slang word *kraut* was used to refer to German sailors, and ultimately all German soldiers, because of the long history of German ships being outfitted with sauerkraut as part of their daily food rations to prevent scurvy. The British also took sauerkraut on their voyages, but later, as they switched to limes, they became known as *limeys*.

FLOATIES TRAP: KEEP LOOSE BITS FROM FLOATING TO THE SURFACE

A *floaties trap* is placed directly on top of the packed cabbage mixture in your jar to trap loose bits trying to float to the surface, where they become a magnet for molds. Here are some suggestions on what to use for a floaties trap:

CABBAGE LEAF

Your easiest and most readily available option is a clean outer leaf from your head of cabbage, torn to size.

PARCHMENT PAPER

A strip of parchment paper—ideally unbleached, so you are not introducing bleaching agents into your sauerkraut—folded to size.

PLASTIC LID

You can also cut the lid from a yogurt tub down to size, using the rim of your jar as a pattern.

FERMENTATION WEIGHT: PREVENT FERMENTING SAUERKRAUT FROM HEAVING

One of the key factors for successful fermentation is keeping everything below the brine. With a packed, shredded ferment—as in sauerkraut—this can be rather difficult, because the gases produced by the bacteria in the first stage of fermentation can't always find their way up and out of the jar and instead accumulate in the packed sauerkraut, causing the mixture to expand and move up and out of the brine. This is called *heaving.*

You have to either place something heavy on top of your ferment (a *fermentation weight*) or put something in the neck of the jar that your expanding sauerkraut is not able to push past. This ensures that your packed ferment stays below the surface of the brine.

The drawback to a fermentation weight is that sometimes enough gases build up in your ferment to actually move the weight up and out of the brine.

Here are some suggestions for a fermentation weight that you may have around your home:

JAR FILLED WITH WATER AND TIGHTLY CAPPED

A jar filled with water and tightly capped was my weight of choice for a few years. Find a jar that will fit in the opening of your fermentation jar. Fill it with water and screw the lid on tight. It will stick out the top of your jar and expose the top of your brine to the air, where molds and yeast could potentially grow, though I rarely experienced this.

MINI JAR

A small jar—without a lid—is placed on top of your ferment, and then the lid for your fermentation vessel is screwed on. The jar is not intended to act as a weight but instead functions as a locked gate. As your ferment expands and moves upward, the small jar is pushed up against the lid and the sauerkraut can go no further. Built-up CO_2 gases are forced out of your sauerkraut and your sauerkraut remains below the brine.

Similar ideas would be a shot glass, baby food jar, espresso cup, small dessert ramekin, or condiment dish. Make sure it fits in the opening of your jar and that you are able to easily remove it.

A major drawback, however, is that the mini jar takes up quite a bit of space that would be better used for brine.

ZIPLOCK BAG FILLED WITH BRINE

The use of a Ziplock bag filled with brine is a common no-cost method for holding ferments below the brine. You start with an empty bag, press it down on your ferment, fill it with brine, and then fold its edges over the rim of your jar. The weight of the brine in the bag holds your ferment below the brine and gases can still work their way out of the jar.

SMALL HEAVY ITEMS

A clean rock or stone (boil for 15 minutes before first using) of the right size can also function as a weight. Small food-safe weights, such as ceramic pie weights or whiskey stones, can be put into a cotton tea bag or plastic Ziploc bag. I would caution against the use of marbles and glass floral gems, since they are not designed for food and it is unknown whether they contain lead or not.

THE FIDDLE METHOD

You can also just keep an eye on your ferment and, when you see it poking up above the surface of your brine, either use a clean fork to push it back down or slide in a wooden skewer or knife down along the side of the jar. Bubbles will rise to the surface. You will probably only have to do this during the first few days of fermentation, when the Bad Gas Gang is hard at work producing gases that push your ferment up and out of the brine.

Here are some suggestions for fermentation weights to purchase with additional details and other options on my Shop page at this shortened URL: **fmeasy.me/shop**

GLASS WEIGHTS

MasonTops was the first company to bring glass weights to the market, with copycat companies following suit. Their weights are made of non-iridized soda glass, which is completely inert and guarantees that no other substances leach into your ferment.

PICKLE HELIX BY TRELLIS & CO.

The Pickle Helix is a length of stainless steel wound into a spring that you place on top of your packed ferment. It automatically adjusts to changing ferment volumes and compresses down to the mere thickness of a glass weight if necessary.

PICKLE PUSHER BY THE ULTIMATE PICKLE JAR

A Pickle Pusher is a silicone disc with a tab-like apron, designed to sit in the neck of your canning jar with the sticky silicone tabs keeping it in place. The addition of a stainless steel rod holds it at a set height and prevents it from tipping.

It occupies very little space, allowing plenty of room for brine. Its one drawback is that your jar has to be packed to a set height for it to effectively work. However, if it doesn't quite sit on your packed ferment, leave it be. Your ferment will most likely expand in the first few days and work its way up to the level of the Pickle Pusher.

CANNING BUDDIES BY VISCODISC

ViscoDisc Canning Buddies are round discs made from food-safe plastic. A disc is inserted into the neck of your jar, where it is held in place with tabs. Canning Buddies occupy very little space, allowing plenty of room for brine. Their one drawback is that your jar has to be packed to a set height for it to effectively work. However, if it doesn't quite sit on your packed ferment, I found that it also works if pushed down into and below the neck of the jar.

FERMENTATION LID: LET GASES ESCAPE AND PREVENT AIR FROM ENTERING

Not only do you need a way for gases to escape but you also want to prevent oxygen, bacteria, mold spores, and wild yeasts from entering your jar.

The *surface* of your ferment is under the brine and will be aerobic, but to reduce the chance of molds and yeasts developing on the surface, we seal the jar with a lid. The type of lid you use will determine how much airflow there is.

LIDS *WITHOUT* AN AIR LOCK

Lids without air locks can be used both for fermentation and for storage, and offer a low-cost entry into small-jar fermentation. Their only drawback is that during the first week, you have to either leave the lid a tad loose or burp it daily to let the gases escape. With this setup, some air can still enter your jar.

METAL LID AND RIM

The metal lids and rims that are included in the purchase of a case of canning jars, or the lid for the used jar you might be recycling, work just fine. However, with the acid created during the fermentation process, these mixed-metal lids will eventually corrode, especially if there is a nick in the lid.

PLASTIC STORAGE CAPS

Storage caps are one-piece lids sold with or without a rubber or silicone sealing gasket. These lids are sold in the same section as canning supplies. I like their clean look andaffordability, and the simplicity of a one-piece lid. This is the lid I use in my teaching recipe and when giving workshops. I also use these lids when storing my sauerkraut.

LIDS *WITH* AN AIR LOCK

An air lock is a one-way valve that allows gases created during fermentation (hydrogen, methane, and carbon dioxide) to escape, while preventing oxygen, bacteria, and wild yeasts in the air from entering your jar and causing your ferment to mold or spoil. These lids form an airtight seal and you do not need to leave the lid loose or burp the jar.

There are various styles of air locks available for wide-mouth canning jars. You may be most familiar with the plastic three-piece water-filled air lock, commonly used by nearly all wine and beer makers. Also available are low-profile waterless air locks, and even water-sealed fermentation lids. A complete list of available products, with additional details, is maintained and kept up to date on my Shop page at this shortened URL: **fmeasy.me/shop**

THREE-PIECE WATER-FILLED CUP AIR LOCKS

The three-piece water-filled cup air locks are quite effective, inexpensive, and readily available. The air lock cup is inserted into a hole drilled in your lid that has been outfitted with a silicone or rubber grommet. The air lock is partially filled with water, an inner cap is placed over the tube inside, and then a secondary cap is popped on. Gases work their way out of your

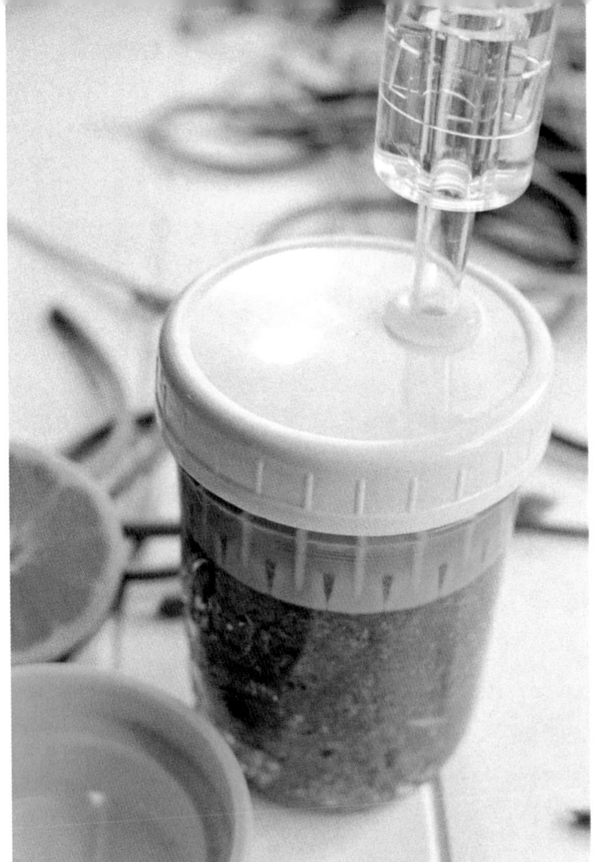

ferment, up the open pipe, and into the water in the air lock. From there, they rise to the surface and escape through pinholes in the lid. No air can enter the jar. Gases can escape. The Sauer System by Fermentology and the Fermentation Kit by Quality Reliable Products are two popular examples of three-piece water-filled cup air locks.

ONE-WAY WATERLESS SELF-SEALING AIR LOCK VALVES

A small, low-profile valve is inserted or built into your fermentation lid. They come in a variety of styles and are generally made from silicone. One style of these self-sealing valves is a small cross-hair cut in the silicone that only opens when there is enough pressure in the jar to force it open. Outside pressure closes the seal. This one-way valve lets carbon dioxide escape from your jar but does not allow air from the outside back into the jar. The Pickle Pipe by MasonTops and the

Easy Fermenter by Nourished Essentials are two popular examples of one-way waterless air locks.

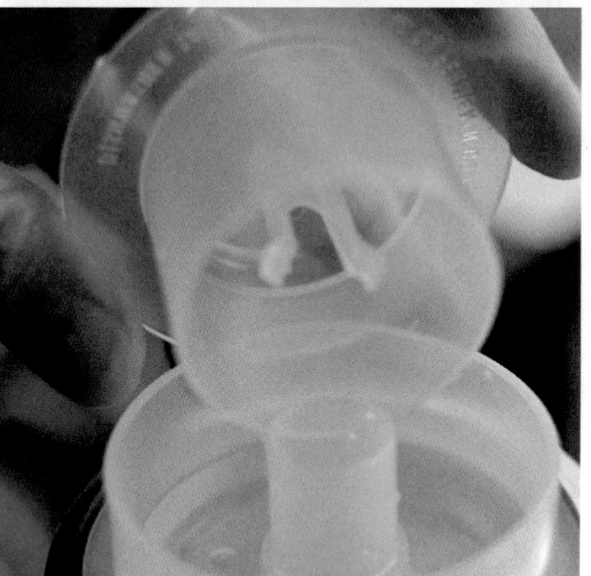

WATER-FILLED FERMENTATION LIDS

Water-sealed fermentation lids work in the same manner as a water-sealed fermentation crock. There is a moat built into your lid that you fill with water, and then a cap or lid is set down into the moat. Gases make their way up and out of your ferment and then bubble up and out through the moat. Oxygen, mold spores, and wild yeast can't work their way into the jar. Your jar is sealed by the use of water. The Fermentation Lid by Kraut Source and the Home Fermentation Kit by Ferment'N are two popular examples of water-filled fermentation lids.

DISPOSABLE GLOVE OR BALLOON

A simple and fun solution. No mess. No fuss. Stretch its opening over the rim of your jar, leaving the fingers to flop to one side. As gases build up, the hand will inflate. To avoid the powder that coats the inside of some gloves, turn the glove inside out before using.

KITCHEN SCALE: YOUR MOST IMPORTANT TOOL

When putting together a batch of sauerkraut, you weigh your ingredients to know how much salt to add. A scale will ensure that you

- slice the right amount of cabbage to fit in your container,
- add the correct amount of salt to your ferment to ensure a safe fermentation,
- make delicious tangy sauerkraut every time, and
- don't waste time and money on cabbage and other ingredients that you had to toss due to the stages of fermentation not properly unfolding.

I recommend a digital scale. Digital scales are more accurate and can easily switch between pounds, ounces, and grams. In addition, a digital scale enables you to measure your salt by weighing it. Since grain sizes vary greatly between salt types and manufacturers, weighing your salt is the most accurate way to add salt to your recipe.

To conserve battery life, most digital scales are programed to automatically shut off after a minute or two, erasing any *tare* reading (the weight of your empty bowl) that you were expecting to make use of. The first time I used my digital scale, I put my bowl on the scale and hit the tare button to set the display to 0 grams; then as I was slicing cabbage, it turned off. When I turned it back on, it no longer knew the weight of my bowl, and I was forced to dump the contents and start the weighing process over.

When using a digital scale with an auto-off feature, make sure you write down the weight of your bowl and add the required cabbage and vegetable weight to that number.

See my Shop page at this shortened URL: **fmeasy.me/shop** for recommended brands, along with directions on how to program my favorite digital scale so that it does not automatically shut off.

SLICING, SHREDDING, AND CHOPPING DEVICES

What you use will affect how easy it is to slice your cabbage, what type of slices you will achieve, and what texture and style of sauerkraut you'll end up with. Start with what you have on hand, but come back here when you are ready to take your sauerkraut to the next level. Changing what you slice with will dictate how easily you are able to achieve thin, even slices of cabbage—the secret to shifting your jar of sauerkraut from a jumbled mass to a work of art, with not only perfect flavor but perfect texture.

KNIVES

When slicing with a chef's knife, it is hard not to end up with some slices that are thick and some that are thin. Once fermented, the thicker ones can be too crunchy and the thinner ones too mushy. Not a crucial factor, but something to be aware of when you're evaluating your knife-sliced sauerkraut and looking for a way to up your game.

CHEF'S KNIFE

Most of us have just the right sized knife for slicing cabbage. A knife with a 10- to 12-inch blade—sometimes called a chef's knife—is great for slicing cabbage. Keep it sharp.

PARING KNIFE

A smaller knife is handy for prepping carrots, garlic, and whatever other flavoring ingredients you may be adding to your batch of sauerkraut.

MANDOLINE OR CABBAGE BOARD

A mandoline is a style of slicer that uses a platform made from wood, plastic, or stainless steel to hold one or more razor-sharp blades. Vegetables are placed on the platform and lightly drawn across the fixed blade, allowing you to slice vegetables not only to a uniform thickness but usually much thinner than you could with a knife.

A precursor to the mandoline, the wooden cabbage shredder (also called kraut cutter, cabbage board, or kraut board) was first devised in the late 1890s. It has three diagonal blades parallel to one another. With each slide of the cabbage over the blades, you get three thin slices. Once you get a good rhythm going, slicing becomes super-efficient. A complete coverage of mandolines can be found on my Shop page at this shortened URL: **fmeasy.me/mandoline**

Although it requires less skill to slice vegetables with a mandoline than with a knife, mandolines can be very dangerous, as the angled blades can quickly slice the tip of your finger. Because of this, most mandolines come with a safety guard to protect your hand. For added safety, consider using cut-resistant safety gloves, which are made from a synthetic fabric that is strong, durable, and cut and puncture resistant.

FOOD PROCESSOR

I pull out my food processor when I'm prepping vegetables for a large batch of sauerkraut that will be fermenting in my 5- or 10-liter water-sealed fermentation crock. I use it to grate large quantities of carrots, radish, and whatnot, or to mince a big handful of garlic cloves.

HAND GRATERS, MICROPLANES, AND VEGETABLE PEELERS

You'll want to have on hand a grater and peeler of some sort for the recipes that call for grated carrots or beets. I find that a microplane works best for zesting citrus fruits, though the fine side of a grater can also get the job done.

OTHER FERMENTATION SUPPLIES

LARGE MIXING BOWL

Most likely, you will have a large mixing bowl in your kitchen that will work fine for mixing your sliced cabbage, vegetables, seasonings, and salt. I prefer glass, though stainless steel or plastic works just fine. Do not use bowls made from aluminum or copper, because the salt used in fermentation quickly reacts with these metals, possibly leaching unwelcome toxins into your sauerkraut.

Your bowl should be large enough to get your hands into, and to mix your sliced cabbage without the contents spilling out onto your counter. A bowl that is wide and shallow works better than one that is tall and narrow.

FREE BOOK BONUS

To download a current list of My Favorite Sauerkraut-Making Tools and Supplies, visit this shortened URL: **fmeasy.me/mwsk**

KRAUT POUNDER

A kraut pounder is a tool used for pounding salted cabbage to release its natural juices, for packing cabbage firmly into your jar or ceramic crock, or for packing finished sauerkraut from a large crock into individual jars for storage. Your hand will do the job just fine, as will a large spoon, the end of a rolling pin, or a meat tenderizer mallet.

Kraut pounders are usually wooden, and sized to fit into wide-mouth canning jars. You can also purchase larger ones for use in crocks. Since wood can easily dry and crack, wash your kraut pounder after using it, dry it immediately, and then rub it with a thin coat of coconut oil or a food-grade mineral oil.

MASKING TAPE AND MARKERS

Please, please, please label your ferments. It is so easy to forget when you started any particular batch. Not only is it handy to have the date on the jar so you can gauge when to stop fermentation, but when you are enjoying the delicious stuff, it is nice to know how long you fermented the particular batch you especially love.

I recommend painter's tape over traditional masking tape because it leaves no residue and is easy to remove. Label the tape with the specific flavor you're fermenting, along with the date it was started. When it is done fermenting, add the fermentation time.

PART 3

Ferment It!

Did you jump right to this section, anxious to ferment your first batch of sauerkraut? No worries, all you need to know to make your first batch of sauerkraut is right here in my teaching recipe. The rest of the book can be read at your leisure, and it will give you that deeper understanding of what is taking place in that jar of yours.

Questions from tens of thousands of readers working their way through my recipes on my blog have helped to refine this recipe. I've got you covered.

I'll take you through the process of making a batch of sauerkraut. Numerous photos, notes, and tips are here to ensure that you will be successful. And if by chance something does go wrong, my comprehensive Troubleshooting Guide (p.57) has you covered. Take joy in the fact that in just a few short weeks you'll be enjoying a flavorful batch of fermented sauerkraut. And, not too many batches after, you'll be able to proclaim, as one of my readers has:

Thanks to your detailed recipe and warm guidance, I can now make sauerkraut in my sleep.

CHAPTER 8

Small-Batch Fermentation Teaching Recipe

The best way to learn how to make sauerkraut is with a simple 1-quart (1 L) jar. Your start-up costs are low, you can watch and monitor the transformation of salty cabbage into sour sauerkraut, and if by chance a batch is ruined, there is very little to throw out.

This is my teaching recipe, and it includes step-by-step photos, numerous tips, and many helpful gems to ensure that you are able to fearlessly ferment your first jar of sauerkraut. I recommend that you scan through the entire recipe before you start. Then carefully work through each step, first reading the "Tips to Make Fermenting a Breeze" section for that step.

STEP 1: SET UP. GATHER SUPPLIES AND SET UP SCALE

For this first step, you will be buying what produce you need and pulling together the necessary equipment.

Even though there are many fancy—and quite effective—weights and air locks to make fermentation easier, you can start with readily found items. If you own some fermentation weights and air locks, by all means use them. If not, wait until you have fermented a few batches, have gained some knowledge and experience, and have developed a bit of fermentation intuition. Then you'll know what additional equipment will work for your household needs and your fermentation preferences.

PURCHASE INGREDIENTS

In this teaching recipe, we make Sweet Garlic Sauerkraut, cabbage lightly seasoned with carrots and garlic. It's a popular flavor, even for children, and it doesn't require any hard-to-find ingredients. If you prefer to ferment cabbage on its own, follow the recipe, omitting the carrots and garlic. And though they are not listed here, you'll also be adding billions of hardworking bacteria. They hitched a free ride on the vegetables, and without them we would not be able to make sauerkraut.

- 1 medium head fresh green cabbage, 2–3 pounds (1 kg)
- 2–3 carrots
- 2–3 cloves garlic
- 1 level tablespoon (15 ml) iodine-free salt

GATHER EQUIPMENT

- Kitchen scale, ideally digital
- 1-quart (1 L) wide-mouth canning jar or similar sized jar
- 4-ounce (125 ml) canning jar (jelly jar) or other fermentation weight
- Wide-mouth plastic storage cap or canning jar rim and lid
- Cutting board and chef's knife
- Large mixing bowl
- Vegetable peeler, measuring spoons, and grater
- Kraut pounder (optional)

SET UP YOUR SCALE

Since you don't want to include the weight of your bowl in your measurements, you need to know its weight, or *tare*. In Step 2: Chop, you will add 1¾ pounds (28 oz or 800 g) to this number.

Place your bowl on the scale. Zero out the scale (for a digital scale, press the "tare" button; for a mechanical scale, turn the small knob under the tray) *or* write down the tare weight.

Note: If you are using a digital scale that automatically shuts off after a few minutes—most do—you will want to write down the weight of your empty bowl.

TIPS TO MAKE FERMENTING A BREEZE

- **Use green cabbage.** You'll have the greatest success if you are able to use the traditional round-headed green cabbage for your first few batches of sauerkraut. Different types of cabbage ferment at different rates.
- **Use a scale.** I highly recommend that you weigh your cabbage and vegetables to ensure that you use the right amount of salt. Fermentation best unfolds at a set range of brine salinity. By using a scale to weigh your ingredients, you ensure that the correct amount of salt is used in your ferment, plus it gives you a base number from which to tweak future batches.
- **The actual volume of tablespoons varies from country to country.** An Australian tablespoon is defined as 20.0 milliliters; British, 17.7 milliliters; and American, 14.7 milliliters. Adjust as necessary, or instead weigh your salt as described in Appendix 2: How Much Salt Do I Add? (p.131).
- **Choose a fermentation weight.** If you don't have access to a 4-ounce (125 ml) canning jar or a similar small jar, see the Fermentation Weight (p.34) section for other suggestions.
- **Make sure your salt does not contain iodine**, sugar, or anti-caking agents that may interfere with the fermentation process. See chapter 6: Salt (p.26) for further information. Himalayan pink salt (fine grain) was used for all recipes in this book.
- **You do not need to sterilize** your jars or equipment for fermentation, just wash well with dishwashing liquid and rinse thoroughly.

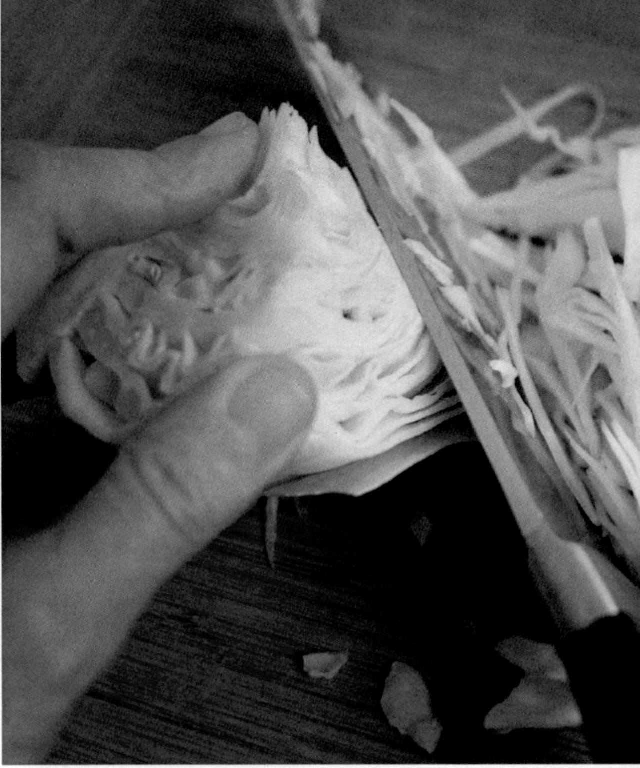

STEP 2: CHOP. CHOP YOUR VEGETABLES AND CABBAGE

Now that you have everything you need on hand and your scale is ready for weighing, it's time to prepare those vegetables for fermentation.

You will need 1¾ pounds (28 oz or 800 g) of vegetables *and* cabbage in your bowl. You first prepare and place the flavoring ingredients—carrots and garlic—in your bowl, then add sliced cabbage. This allows you to add only as much sliced cabbage as necessary to hit 1¾ pounds on the scale.

Why? 1¾ pounds (28 oz or 800 g) is the perfect amount of cabbage and vegetables to mix with 1 tablespoon of salt, creating the right saltiness of brine to ensure perfectly fermented sauerkraut. And it's also the perfect amount of sauerkraut to pack into a 1-quart (1 L) jar.

Prep carrots and garlic. Peel and grate two to three carrots. Add these to the bowl. Finely mince two to three garlic cloves and add these to the bowl, too.

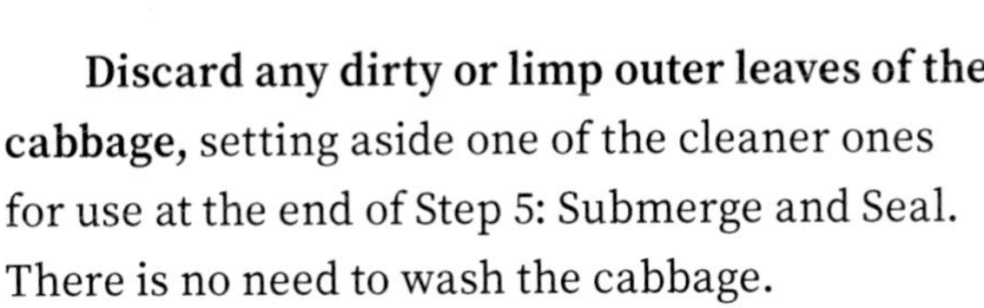

Discard any dirty or limp outer leaves of the cabbage, setting aside one of the cleaner ones for use at the end of Step 5: Submerge and Seal. There is no need to wash the cabbage.

Slice your cabbage. Quarter the cabbage, leaving the core in, though you won't end up actually slicing the core. Place a cabbage quarter on one of its sides and slice the cabbage crosswise. Aim for narrow ribbons, which will produce liquid faster—and ferment more quickly—than wider-cut ribbons. Slice until just the core remains.

Add sliced cabbage to your bowl until the weight of your vegetables and cabbage is 1¾ pounds (28 oz or 800 g). I find it easiest to work in grams.

Wow! The big job of grating, slicing, and weighing is done! You are now ready for the magic: creating the brine in which the Mighty Microbes will set up camp and ferment your sauerkraut for you.

TIPS TO MAKE FERMENTING A BREEZE

- **You don't need to wash.** Washing vegetables is a personal choice and is generally not necessary. Remove damaged leaves, cut out bad spots, and give them a quick rinse if they have dirt clinging to them. Definitely not necessary are vinegar solutions, vegetable washes, or rinsing with hot water.
- **You don't need to peel.** I'm a peeler, though I probably shouldn't be. The greatest concentration of bacteria resides in the peels of root vegetables (the part that comes in contact with the dirt where those little buggers live). By peeling the carrot, you might be hindering the process of fermentation.
- **Leave the cabbage core in place.** I find it easier to slice my cabbage if the core is not removed. It serves to hold the layers of cabbage together, making the job of slicing easier, and gives you something to hold onto while slicing. I don't use the core but instead feed it to the worms in my compost pile.

- **Stay away from large chunks.** When slicing cabbage and preparing other vegetables for sauerkraut, the idea is to expose as much surface area as possible, to pull out the juices and create a brine. When ingredients are too large, especially with dense vegetables like carrots, it's difficult for the lactic acid to get inside them.
- **You can use a food processor for slicing.** Some fermenters love to use a food processor to slice their cabbage. The 2-millimeter slicing disk or the "large" grater disk will result in nicer slices than the S-blade. If you use the S-blade, be sure not to overprocess the cabbage.
- **You can use a mandoline for slicing.** My top recommendation for slicing would be a wide-body mandolin, for effortlessly creating ribbon-like strands of cabbage. Currently recommended brands can be found on my Shop page at this shortened URL: **fmeasy.me/mandoline**
- **Follow the 25–75 rule.** If you are unsure of how many carrots to grate, keep approximately 25% of the total weight as flavoring ingredients (carrots, garlic, onions, etc.) and the remaining 75% as sliced cabbage. This makes for a nice flavor balance and a healthy ferment. That means your flavorings will weigh approximately 7 ounces (200 g) and your cabbage 21 ounces (600 g).

STEP 3: SALT. CREATE YOUR BRINE

This is the stage where you create the brine in which your sauerkraut will ferment. Believe it or not, that big bowl of sliced cabbage really will fit into your jar.

To make your brine, you need salt. Salt pulls water out of the cells in the cabbage and vegetables (through osmosis) to create an environment where the good, salt-loving bacteria can grow and proliferate and the bad, salt-phobic bacteria die off.

Sprinkle vegetables and cabbage with 1 tablespoon (15 ml) of salt—16 grams, if weighing—and mix well. Don't rush this step. You want to ensure that the salt is evenly distributed. For me, once I'm sure it is well mixed, I stop and clean up my work space. By leaving the salted cabbage to sit in the bowl while I do so, I'm letting the salt start to pull the moisture out of the cabbage, making the next task simple and rather pleasurable.

Massage and squeeze the vegetables with strong hands until moist, creating the brine. The mixture will shrink in size and want to clump together. You should be able to tilt the bowl to the side and see a good-sized puddle of brine, about 2–3 inches (5–8 cm) in diameter. This process can take anywhere from 2 to 10 minutes.

It doesn't hurt to take a few nibbles of the mixture as you work. You'll have a base flavor sensation for what a salted cabbage mixture tastes like before it ferments.

TIPS TO MAKE FERMENTING A BREEZE

- **Use fresh cabbage.** The fresher the cabbage and the higher the moisture content, the quicker the brine will be created. If you're making sauerkraut in the fall with fresh cabbage, you'll see this for sure. On the other hand, if you're making sauerkraut with cabbage that has been stored for months, you'll find it harder to create the brine and there'll be less of it.
- **Weigh your salt.** If you have a digital scale and the personality for exactness, you can use your scale to weigh the correct amount of salt. For a batch of 1¾ pounds (28 oz or 800 g), add 16 grams of salt. Weighing your salt also negates volume differences due to grain size.

STEP 4: PACK. PACK MIXTURE INTO JAR

Your big bowl of cabbage and carrots has now shrunk to a manageable, moist mass. The brine that was created will keep your sauerkraut safe from harmful bacteria while it is fermenting. It's time to pack the cabbage mixture into your jar.

Grab handfuls of the salty, juicy cabbage mixture and pack it into your 1-quart (1 L) wide-mouth canning jar, periodically pressing the mixture down firmly with your fist or a large spoon so that the brine rises above the top of the mixture and no air pockets remain. If you have a sauerkraut pounder, now is a good time to put it to use.

To give space for brine and also allow for expansion as carbon dioxide increases during fermentation, be sure to leave at least 1–2 inches between the top of the packed cabbage and the top of the jar. Because we weighed out just the right amount of cabbage to fit in your jar, this should happen automatically.

Pour any brine left in your mixing bowl into the jar and scrape out any loose bits stuck to the sides of the bowl.

Lastly, wipe down the outside of the jar and push down any tidbits on the inside of the jar that may remain above your packed ferment.

TIPS TO MAKE FERMENTING A BREEZE

- **Pack your jar tightly, but not too tightly.** Apply enough pressure as you're packing to remove visible air pockets, but not so much that it feels like you might break the jar.
- **Use packing tools if necessary.** If your hand is too large to fit into the jar, a kraut pounder can be used, or a large spoon, the end of a rolling pin, or a meat pounder.
- **Avoid a mess.** When packing your jar, it helps to hold the jar in one hand (a clean hand) and pack with the other, holding everything over the bowl. This helps to keep the mess manageable. Some readers find a wide-mouth canning funnel useful for filling their jars.
- **Not enough brine to cover your packed sauerkraut?** See my Troubleshooting Guide (p.57) for ways to add moisture to your mixture.

STEP 5: SUBMERGE AND SEAL. HOLD BELOW BRINE

Now that your jar has been packed with that beautiful cabbage mixture, you need to make sure it remains submerged in the brine throughout fermentation, safe from harm.

You will use a **floaties trap** to keep small bits from floating to the surface, a **fermentation weight** to prevent your packed mixture from moving up and out of the jar, and a **lid** to both allow gases created by the bacteria to escape and prevent additional air from entering your jar.

Floaties trap. Take that cabbage leaf you saved in Step 2: Chop and tear it down to just fit in the jar. Or be a bit obsessive and trace the jar lid on the cabbage leaf, then cut it to size. Place over the surface of the packed cabbage.

Fermentation weight. To hold the vegetables below the brine, place the 4-ounce jelly jar (or your weight of choice) on top of the cabbage leaf, right side up with its lid removed. It might stick out of the top of the jar a bit, but don't worry—when you screw on the lid, it will get pressed down into place.

Lid. Lightly screw the white plastic storage lid onto the jar. Leaving the lid a bit loose allows for the escape of the CO_2 gases that will build up during the first few days of fermentation.

If you have lots of brine in the jar, you may need to pour some of it out to get the lid on without the liquid overflowing.

TIPS TO MAKE FERMENTING A BREEZE

- **No floaties trap?** If you forgot to save a cabbage leaf for your floaties trap, sift through your cabbage scraps and see if you can retrieve one. If that doesn't pan out, fold a narrow piece of parchment paper to size or cut an old plastic lid (from a yogurt tub, perhaps) to size.
- **No jelly jar?** If you don't have access to a small jelly jar for a weight, look around your kitchen for another small jar, a shot glass, or perhaps one of those small jars that mushrooms or pimentos are sold in. Some use a clean rock. You can also use a food-grade freezer bag filled with salt water: 1 tablespoon (15 ml) salt to 2 cups (480 ml) water.
- **Not enough brine to cover your packed sauerkraut?** Go ahead and put the lid on your jar and check it in one day. If there is still not enough brine, dissolve 1 tablespoon (15 ml) salt in 2 cups (480 ml) water and pour in until packed mixture is covered.

STEP 6: FERMENT. FERMENT FOR 2 TO 4 WEEKS

Now sit back and relax as the friendly bacteria eat the sugars in the cabbage and carrots, multiply, and release copious amounts of lactic acid, which creates an environment inhospitable to pathogenic bacteria, acts as a natural preservative for your ferment, and gives your sauerkraut that familiar tang.

DAY ONE: SET THE STAGE FOR SUCCESS

Label your artwork. Label your jar with the flavor of sauerkraut you made and the date you started fermenting it.

Place your jar of fermenting sauerkraut in a shallow bowl to catch any brine that may leak out during the first week of fermentation.

Find the right spot. You'll want a location that fulfills the following criteria:

- **It's out of direct sunlight.** The high levels of ultraviolet radiation in *direct* sunlight can destroy or inhibit the bacteria that will be working for you and can also diminish nutrients in the food that is being fermented. I keep all my jar ferments in my kitchen on the counter, where I can monitor their progress.
- **It's away from excess heat.** Find a spot away from your stove or your refrigerator, due to the excess heat these appliances generate.

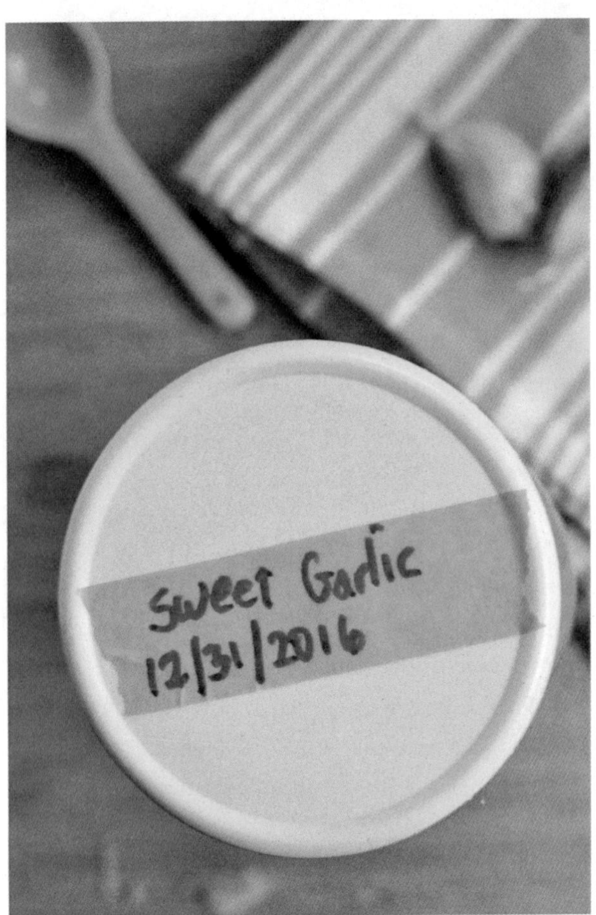

- **It's within the ideal temperature range.** The ideal fermentation temperature for producing sauerkraut with the most complex flavors is between 65 and 70 °F (18–21 °C). Ideally, you want the temperature to be somewhat stable, not fluctuating more than 5 °F (3 °C) in either direction.

THE FIRST WEEK: WHAT TO KEEP AN EYE OUT FOR

Within a day or two, you should see little champagne-like bubbles slowly moving through the sauerkraut and rising to the surface. The brine in your sauerkraut may slowly change from clear to cloudy, and you may notice some white sediment forming at the bottom of the jar.

Release trapped gases. If you are using a lid without an air lock, either leave the lid a tad loose or loosen it until you hear a slight hiss. Then retighten your lid.

For most of the first week, you'll notice plenty of brine, and your packed sauerkraut should remain under this brine. However, you may observe that the level of the brine moves up and down throughout the day, due to changes in the ambient temperature.

WEEKS TWO THROUGH FOUR: ALL IS QUIET

After the first week, you may see the brine level drop and the upper part of your sauerkraut become exposed. This is normal, especially in the small environment of a jar, and happens when the active stage of fermentation is complete. No need to worry. Lactic acid levels have reached a high enough concentration to prevent pathogenic bacteria from taking hold.

HOW LONG TO FERMENT?

If your home environment is within the ideal temperature range, 3–4 weeks is a good length of time to ferment your sauerkraut. However, if you have home temperatures at the high end, 70–75 °F (21–24 °C), fermentation can take just 10 days to 2 weeks. If home temperatures are at the cool end, 60–65 °F (16–18 °C), fermentation can take 4–6 weeks.

HOW TO KNOW WHEN IT'S DONE: WHAT SHOULD MY SAUERKRAUT LOOK, SMELL, FEEL, AND TASTE LIKE?

Wait until at least day 7–10, then pop the lid on your jar of sauerkraut. Take a whiff, then carefully remove your weight and floaties trap and grab a forkful for evaluation.

- **Color.** No longer bright green, but instead pale green or even yellow. Strands will also appear somewhat translucent.
- **Smell.** Slightly sour, perhaps reminiscent of vinegar. This sour smell indicates that the pH has dropped and plenty of lactic acid has been produced.
- **Texture.** Squeeze some sauerkraut between your fingers. If it squeaks, be happy. That's a good sign. The texture of your sauerkraut can vary from crisp and crunchy to soggy and soft, depending on duration and temperature of fermentation. There is a personal preference here. I like a bit of a crunch; others are looking for a soft texture.
- **Taste.** Slightly sour, with a bite to it that may remind you of vinegar. Tangy. It will taste a bit salty, but not as salty as when you first packed your jar. It should have complex notes, with a flavor that makes you go, *Wow*, this is good!

FREE BOOK BONUS

Free DOWNLOAD

To download a Fermentation Checklist, handy for monitoring your ferment as the bacteria work for you, visit this shortened URL: **fmeasy.me/mwsk**

TIPS TO MAKE FERMENTING A BREEZE

- **Disappearing brine.** If the brine in your jar seems to suddenly disappear, don't panic. This can be due to a few things. Cooler temperatures can pull the brine back into the sauerkraut. When the house warms up, brine levels usually rise again. Atmospheric pressure will also affect brine levels.
- **Trapped air bubbles.** If air bubbles get trapped in your sauerkraut, the mixture will expand and force your fermentation weight up, making it look like there is no brine. Open your jar and gently press the mixture back down under the brine.
- **Music.** You will hear an occasional fizzy sound from air escaping the jar. This is normal, and is caused by carbon dioxide escaping the jar. It is one sign that fermentation is happening.

STEP 7: STORE. STORE IN REFRIGERATOR FOR UP TO ONE YEAR

After your sauerkraut has fermented to your liking, it's time to move it to cold storage until you are ready to effortlessly add its probiotic-rich flavors to your meals.

The ideal temperature at which to store sauerkraut is 35–38 °F (2–3 °C), which happens to be the typical temperature of a refrigerator. With these temperatures, you won't notice much change in the texture over a 12-month period, the typical storage duration for sauerkraut. If you store your sauerkraut in a cool basement, at around 55 °F (13 °C), storage duration should be reduced and texture will soften.

If space is at a premium, you can find a variety of ways to store sauerkraut on my website at this shortened URL: **fmeasy.me/store**

Wherever stored, your sauerkraut will continue to ferment—aging like a fine wine—at a rate based on storage temperature. Flavors shift and deepen over time. If successfully fermented, your sauerkraut can be kept preserved in your refrigerator for a year or even longer.

Rinse off the outside of the jar and remove the little jar, or whatever weight you used. Leave the cabbage leaf in place until you start eating from your jar of sauerkraut. Clean any sticky brine off the rim and jar, and screw the lid back on tightly. If you used a special air lock lid, replace it with a simple lid. I like to use the white plastic storage lids for storing my sauerkraut.

Add the fermentation time to your label. It is always nice to know how long a batch fermented, so you can adjust for future batches.

Place at a handy location in your refrigerator. Seeing your jar of sauerkraut when you open the refrigerator is a nice reminder to add it to your meal.

Enjoy! When trying to incorporate sauerkraut into your diet, keep it simple by just adding a forkful or two to your meals. For more simple ways to enjoy your sauerkraut, go to Chapter 15: Effortlessly Adding Sauerkraut to Any Meal (p.123).

CHAPTER 9

Troubleshooting Guide

Fermenting your own sauerkraut is a fun and educational way to make delicious foods, but every once in a while something may go wrong, even for the best of us. Mold grows, fruit flies invade, or the odors emanating from your jar are simply too noxious. Follow these tips to fix your current batch if possible, or to fine-tune future batches. You'll be amazed at the education you will receive from the inhabitants of our microscopic world.

THINGS GROWING ON MY SAUERKRAUT

The sudden invasion of green and black fuzz (mold) or a white powder (Kahm yeast) on your ferment can be rather alarming, prompting even the hardiest of us to toss it all and vow to never ferment again.

KAHM YEAST

Kahm can describe a number of yeasts that can appear on the surface of a ferment that hasn't reached a high enough acidity. Kahm yeast is a flat, thin, white- to cream-colored powder, and if it grows thick enough, it can almost look like velvet. The smell of Kahm yeast can range from yeasty to cheesy, or even be reminiscent of alcohol.

Kahm yeast appears most often during warm weather and when fermenting sweeter vegetables, such as beets, carrots, and peppers.

Kahm yeast is harmless, but it can impart an off taste to a ferment.

Ferment at cooler temperatures. This is especially important during the first few days of fermentation. Look around your home for a cooler spot with a temperature range of 65–70 °F (18–21 °C).

Use sufficient salt. It can be a good idea to increase the amount of salt when fermenting at temperatures that are higher than ideal. Use a heaping tablespoon instead of a level tablespoon, or if weighing your salt, 2.5% of your vegetables' weight.

Finely slice cabbage. A fast rise of acidity levels in your jar reduces the chance that Kahm yeast will take hold. Acid levels rise as the bacteria consume the naturally occurring sugars in your cabbage and vegetables, sugars that are locked inside the cells of your vegetables. By thinly slicing your cabbage, you make it easier for the bacteria to get at those sugars.

Keep your ferment submerged and sealed. Since yeasts are airborne and can only grow where there is air, be sure to submerge your ferment below the brine and use a lid on your fermentation vessel.

WHAT TO DO IF YOU HAVE KAHM YEAST GROWING ON YOUR FERMENT

Due to its powdery nature, Kahm yeast can be hard to remove, and once it has invaded your jar, it tends to reappear after removal, even when stored in your refrigerator. Skim off the yeast as it appears, including what is stuck to the jar. When your ferment is done, taste the top layer. If it tastes yeasty, remove layer by layer until you get down to a section that tastes fine. Then repack your sauerkraut into a clean jar.

This is a time to thoroughly clean your jar and lid, perhaps using a distilled white vinegar solution.

MOLD

Mold is raised and fuzzy and can be white, black, blue, green, or even pink. Mold grows from mold spores that are present everywhere in the air and on the surface of fruits and vegetables. Mold begins growing when spores land—or already exist—on a wet, nutrient-rich *surface*, such as a bit of exposed cabbage, and over time grows into a thick layer. Spores can actually survive in acidic foods, so it's not necessarily the acidity that deters them.

Use clean equipment. Clean does not mean sterile. Simply clean your jars and equipment with a gentle dishwashing liquid and rinse well with water.

Pack jar 75–80% full. Too much air in your jar can lead to mold growth. Ideally, you want to size your batches so that they fill your container about three-quarters full, to decrease the amount of air in the jar.

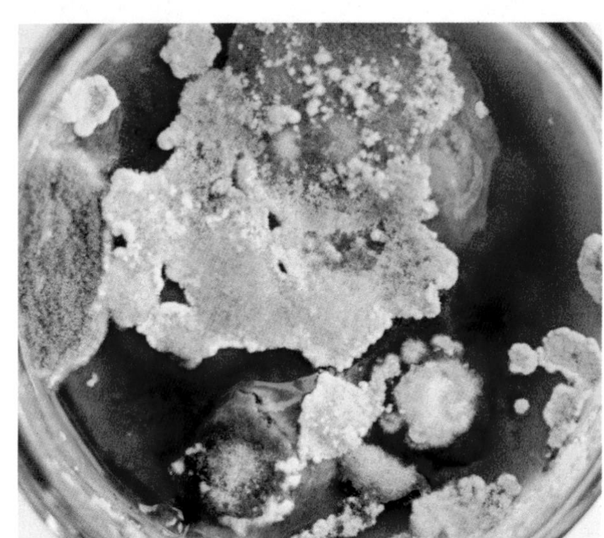

Ferment at cooler temperatures. This is especially important during the first few days of fermentation. Look around your home for a cooler spot at a temperature range of 65–70 °F (18–21 °C).

Use sufficient salt. If you're fermenting at temperatures that are higher than ideal, increase the amount of salt you use. Use a heaping tablespoon instead of a level tablespoon, or if weighing your salt, 2.5% of your vegetables' weight.

Use fresh, quality ingredients. Vegetables that are starting to go bad have a higher mold content than fresh vegetables. Give a competitive advantage to the good bacteria and use super-fresh vegetables.

SHOULD YOU SALVAGE A MOLDY FERMENT OR BE SAFE AND TOSS IT?

This is a personal question that you will have to answer. Mold spores are everywhere. We can't eliminate them. If the environment is right, mold spores will grow and multiply on the surface of your ferment wherever the nutrient-rich surface is in contact with oxygen-rich air. Usually, underneath the mold growth your ferment is untouched and smells fresh and clean.

Most find it perfectly safe to remove the layer of mold on top of their ferment. This is fine with greenish or grayish mold. However, toss ferments with black, pink, or orange mold, or if they have an off smell. If you are not comfortable salvaging a ferment or are sensitive to molds, by all means, throw it all out!

HOW TO SALVAGE A FERMENT THAT HAS MOLD

Remove mold as best you can as soon as you see it. The longer you allow the mold to grow, the deeper it penetrates your ferment. Use a large spoon to get under the mold and lift it off. Evaluate the texture of the underlying ferment, removing any layers that are soft or discolored.

BUBBLE ISSUES

During the first few days of fermentation, when the first bacterial strains go to work and produce carbon dioxide, you should see little champagne-like bubbles slowly moving through the sauerkraut and rising to the surface. You may even hear an occasional fizzy sound as the bubbles work their way out of your jar, either through your loose lid or through an air lock.

Though this is one of the key fermentation signs, don't panic and toss your jar if you don't see bubbles. They can be elusive, and not every batch of sauerkraut progresses through each stage with perfect timing.

NO BUBBLES

The bubbles are most likely in your jar but you can't see them because they are trapped within the packed fermentation mixture. If it is past the first 5–7 days, you may no longer see many bubbles, if any.

Release trapped bubbles. To reassure yourself that fermentation is progressing, try a few solid taps on the outside of the jar and watch for bubbles moving up the sides of your jar.

Find a warmer spot. If your home is especially cool, fermentation will unfold slowly and carbon dioxide production will be reduced. Move your jar to a warmer spot: 65–70 °F (18–21 °C).

Check your cabbage source. The amount of bubbles you see depends somewhat on the sugar levels in your cabbage. Cabbage low in sugar provides less food for the bacteria to eat and results in a reduced production of carbon dioxide.

Also be aware that cabbage that has been irradiated to increase its shelf life is devoid of microbial life, the very microbes necessary for fermentation. To avoid this issue, purchase organic cabbage.

FOAM-LIKE MASS OF BUBBLES

With some batches of sauerkraut—usually those exceptionally high in natural sugars—you may see a foam-like mass of bubbles collecting on the surface of your ferment. The bubbles may even be colored if there are pigment-rich vegetables in your sauerkraut. For example, the red pigment in beets will leave a dark-red to brownish scum of bubbles.

Skim off foam. Skim any persistent foam off the surface and discard. Foaming slows down quite quickly and usually stops by the end of the first week.

Reduce the amount of sweet vegetables used. A good rule of thumb for a balanced batch of sauerkraut is 25% flavoring ingredients and 75% cabbage, especially when including sweet ingredients, such as carrots, beets, sweet peppers, and corn.

BRINE ISSUES

Brine, that essential, salty, nutrient-rich fluid that keeps our ferment safe from airborne molds and yeasts. Sometimes it is so copious that it flows out of the jar and onto our countertop. Other times, it just disappears and leaves our sauerkraut high and dry.

BRINE OVERFLOW

The first week of fermentation is when your ferment is most visibly active. Gases created during this first stage of fermentation need to push their way up and out of your packed sauerkraut. If these air bubbles instead get trapped in your packed sauerkraut, the mixture will expand and move up in the jar. This is called *heaving* and results in either brine pushing up and out to make a puddle around the jar or brine trickling down into available air pockets to make the top of your sauerkraut look dry.

Leave enough head space in your jar. Yes, it's easy to overpack a jar trying to avoid wasting any of that precious space. Doing so usually ends in a messy disaster. Pack your jars about 75% full, leaving about 2 inches (5 cm) of space between the top of your packed sauerkraut and the top of your jar.

Release trapped air bubbles. To release these trapped bubbles, first remove the lid, then either push down on the weight, slide a butter knife along the inside of the jar, or poke the sauerkraut with a bamboo skewer. This will release the air bubbles and allow the sauerkraut to condense back down into the jar.

CLOUDY BRINE

Cloudy brine is perfectly normal and actually a sign that fermentation is progressing. You may also notice some white sediment forming at the bottom of the jar. This white powder is created by the bacteria. If your sauerkraut contains beets, turmeric, or other deeply colored vegetables, you may see the brine change to match the color of what you are fermenting.

BROWN BRINE

Brown brine can come from the ingredients in your ferment. When the red color in beets or red cabbage breaks down, it turns brown. Outside of that simple answer, brown brine can result when fermenting in weather too warm for the ideal unfolding of the stages of fermentation. If your ferment still has a fresh odor and a tangy flavor, it is safe to eat.

SLIMY BRINE

Sauerkraut with thick, stringy, slimy brine occasionally develops early on in the fermentation process, due to the production of *dextrans* by rapidly growing strains of *Leuconostoc* bacteria. Dextrans are high-molecular-weight polysaccharides made from glucose molecules, hence the slippery, syrupy brine. This occurs especially at elevated temperatures or when fermenting vegetables high in sugars, like beets, carrots, or sweet peppers.

Ferment at cooler temperatures. This is especially important during the first few days of fermentation. Look around your home for a cooler spot or ferment during a cooler season. A temperature range of 65–70 °F (18–21 °C) is best.

Use fresh ingredients. Slimy brine was present in a recent experimental batch of mine. I had used *very* old cabbage, yellowed and lacking in moisture. The bacteria necessary for an ideal ferment were long gone.

Reduce quantity of high-sugar vegetables. Since slimy brine is most common with high-sugar vegetables, keep them to a minimum.

Give the bacteria some time to rebalance. Place your finished jar of sauerkraut in the refrigerator for a few weeks to give the bacteria a chance to rebalance. Often, the slimy brine disappears.

TOO MUCH BRINE

The amount of brine produced in your fermenting sauerkraut can vary dramatically from one batch to the next. Generally, you'll have more brine at the beginning of fermentation and during the part of the day when your house is warmer.

Leave enough head space in your jar. You'll want to get into the habit of leaving 2 inches (5 cm) of space between the top of your packed sauerkraut and the top of your jar. This gives the brine a place to go as your packed sauerkraut expands.

Use a fermentation weight that takes up less space. I still recommend a little jar as a weight, to keep things simple for first-time fermenters. However, one of its drawbacks is that it uses up space that would be better left for the brine. Some find greater success with purchased glass weights.

Invest in a more effective fermentation weight. Gate-style weights are "locked" into the neck of your jar and can't be moved by the force of the expanding sauerkraut mixture. Your ferment will then remain in place below the brine. Currently available examples of gate-style weights are ViscoDisc Canning Buddies and the Pickle Pusher. Visit my Shop page at this shortened URL: **fmeasy.me/weights**

Some fermentation weights are actual stainless steel springs that use the pressure from a coiled spring to push your ferment down under the brine. Currently available examples of spring-style weights are the Pickle Helix and the Kraut Source Fermentation Lid. Visit my Shop page at this shortened URL: **fmeasy.me/weights**

NOT ENOUGH BRINE

You may notice as you are mixing and massaging the salt into your cabbage that not much liquid is being released. Here are a few ways to ensure you have enough brine.

Use fresh cabbage. Even though cabbage is approximately 92% water, if it is June and you're about to make a batch of sauerkraut, that cabbage has most likely been in cold storage for six months and will have lost some of its moisture. The closer to harvest that you purchase your cabbage—and make sauerkraut—the more brine it will produce and the less chance of dry sauerkraut.

Include watery vegetables. Grated radishes, carrots, or beets and thinly sliced onions or turnips will all give off a lot of liquid and help make copious brine.

Add citrus juice. This tip comes from Kirsten and Christopher Shockey, authors of my favorite fermentation book, *Fermented Vegetables:*

> *A few tablespoons of lemon juice, bottled or fresh, can save the day. The lemon flavor will be subtle, as it gets lost in the acidity that you are creating with the fermentation. If you want to taste the lemon, add the zest also. You can also add fresh-squeezed orange, lime, or grapefruit juice.*

Slice cabbage more thinly. Thin thread-like cuts of cabbage, about ⅛ inch (2–3 mm) thick, make for easy brine production, along with an overall improved quality of the finished product.

Give your freshly salted cabbage a bit of time. Once I have added salt to my cabbage and then mixed it well, I leave it be for 20–30 minutes. By then, the cabbage is glistening with beads of moisture and very little massaging has to be done to get a nice puddle of brine in the bottom of my bowl.

If after massaging for 5 minutes, you find that you still don't have enough brine, give it another hour or so and then consider adding a watery vegetable or a bit of citrus juice as suggested above.

Ferment in a water-sealed crock. When fermenting in a water-sealed ceramic fermentation crock, you generally end up with much more moisture in your finished sauerkraut. This has something to do with the larger environment, the greater stability provided by thick ceramic walls, and the greater amount of microbial activity that takes place in a large crock.

Add more brine. Any time you add salted water (brine) to your sauerkraut, you risk diluting the flavors, upping the sodium levels, softening the texture, and possibly causing discoloration in the finished product. But sometimes the benefits of keeping your ferment covered in brine outweigh those drawbacks. There are three stages during which to consider adding brine.

1. If your sauerkraut is sitting high and dry 24 hours after you packed your jar, add just enough brine to keep your ferment covered for the crucial first week of fermentation.
2. If your sauerkraut looks dry after the first week of fermentation, when the brine-producing bacteria are no longer working, don't feel you need to add brine. A healthy fermentation environment with high levels of lactic acid has been established and you should not see mold growth.
3. If your sauerkraut looks dry when it's time to move it to the refrigerator, or if it's been in the fridge for a day or so and the cold of your refrigerator has pulled the brine back into the cabbage, you can add brine to reduce air exposure. Doing so, however, softens the texture of your sauerkraut and makes it taste somewhat watery.

BRINE CHART

To make brine, stir salt into chlorine-free water and mix well. Don't worry if not all of the salt dissolves. The measurements below are for a 2% brine.

1 cup (250 ml) water–1 heaping teaspoon (5 g) salt

2 cups (500 ml) water–2 heaping teaspoons (10 g) salt

TEXTURE ISSUES

The texture of your finished ferment can range from melt-in-your-mouth soft to hurt-your-teeth crunchy, with everything in between. Variations in batches occur throughout the year, usually due to the temperature at which you are fermenting, along with the freshness of your ingredients.

SAUERKRAUT THAT IS TOO SOFT

Soft sauerkraut results when bacteria that normally do not initiate growth until the later stages of sauerkraut production actually grow earlier, usually due to too-high fermentation temperatures or not enough salt. You can't rescue the current batch, but for future batches, adjust one or all of the following:

- **Salinity.** A higher salinity will slow down fermentation. Bump up your salt numbers just a tad. For a 1-quart (1 L) batch, add a tad more salt: ½ teaspoon (4 g).
- **Temperature.** Ferment at cooler temperatures.
- **Time.** Ferment for a shorter time period. Sample your sauerkraut at the one-week mark and then every few days until it is at your preferred texture.

SAUERKRAUT THAT IS TOO CRUNCHY

To achieve a softer texture, adjust one or all of the following:

- **Salinity.** Use a tad less salt for future batches. For a 1-quart (1 L) batch, use 2½ teaspoons (14 g) total.
- **Temperature.** Ferment at warmer temperatures.
- **Time.** Ferment for a longer time period.
- **Pounding.** When you are making your next batch, once you have mixed in your salt, spend some time actually pounding your cabbage mixture with a kraut pounder to break down the cabbage cells.

FLAVOR ISSUES

Be mindful of how your sauerkraut tastes and gradually refine your fermentation process until you get it right. Life is too short to eat blah sauerkraut!

SAUERKRAUT THAT IS NOT SOUR ENOUGH OR IS LACKING TANG

The sour flavor in sauerkraut comes from lactic acid produced by the lactic acid bacteria (LAB) as they eat the sugars in your cabbage and vegetables. Once all the sugars have been converted to lactic acid, your maximum levels of tang have been reached.

- **Time.** If the cabbage you used wasn't especially sweet, you may not find your sauerkraut to be sour enough a few weeks into the process. Let it ferment a few days longer, then sample once again.
- **Provide more sugar for the LAB.** For future batches under similar conditions, experiment with adding a touch of sugar to your ferment, say ½ teaspoon (2 ml) for a 1-quart (1 L) jar. This will provide more food for the LAB to create higher levels of lactic acid.

SAUERKRAUT THAT IS TOO SALTY

Personal preference, along with the type of salt you use, will play a role in how salty your finished sauerkraut tastes. Also important is the proper movement through the fermentation stages, to develop high levels of a wide range of lactic acid to somewhat mask the saltiness.

- **Use a mineral-rich salt.** Himalayan pink salt and Redmond's Real Salt are mineral-rich salts that contain a bit less sodium and impart a greater depth of flavor to foods than ordinary table salt.
- **Use a bit less salt.** Decrease the amount of salt used to 1.5%, or 2½ teaspoons (12 g).
- **Rinse.** Just before eating, you can give your sauerkraut a quick rinse. This will wash off some but not all of the beneficial bacteria.
- **Disperse the saltiness.** Mix your sauerkraut into a salad or stir it into a dish just before serving.
- **Ferment longer.** Sodium levels in sauerkraut are not changed by fermentation. However, as your sauerkraut ferments, acid levels rise, which will mask the salty taste.
- **Dehydrate.** You can salvage a salty batch of sauerkraut by dehydrating it into a flavoring salt. I use my kimchi flavoring salt in deviled eggs, pasta dishes, and sautéed greens.

COLOR CONCERNS

As sauerkraut ferments, the bright green of the cabbage slowly fades to become almost white at the end of fermentation. This is normal. But what if your sauerkraut turns pink? Or brown?

PINK SAUERKRAUT

Pink sauerkraut can be quite beautiful and is great if it comes from red cabbage, beets, red kale, or even some fruits. But sometimes pink color in sauerkraut is caused by pigments produced by the growth of certain types of yeasts. These yeasts may grow if there is too much salt or an uneven distribution of salt, or if the kraut is insufficiently covered during fermentation. The yeasts that cause pink sauerkraut are not considered harmful and the sauerkraut is perfectly safe to eat.

BROWN SAUERKRAUT

During fermentation. Some notice the top layer of their sauerkraut turning brown during fermentation. This is due to air getting into your ferment. Make sure that you are using a weight to keep everything below the brine.

During storage. Over time, a jar of sauerkraut stored in your refrigerator will darken slightly. This is normal and perfectly fine to eat. However, if there is a brown layer of sauerkraut at the top of the jar, that portion is oxidized. Air got to that section of sauerkraut and caused it to turn brown. Since it is protecting the sauerkraut below, leave it alone. Move your jar to the refrigerator until you are ready to eat from it, then remove and toss the oxidized layer.

SMELL ISSUES

Funky old socks? Gym sweat? Farts? Rotten eggs? Stinky Swiss cheese? Sulfur? Even bleach? The sulfur-containing compounds in cabbage (and other cruciferous vegetables) can produce rather strong and pungent odors. This is normal and does not happen with every batch.

Compare to store-bought sauerkraut. If you are not sure whether the smell is normal, buy a jar of sauerkraut to get a sense of what sauerkraut smells like. Look for raw, unpasteurized sauerkraut in the refrigerated section of a natural foods store.

If your sauerkraut smells like rotting or putrid food, you'll want to toss it. Putrid is an unmistakably awful odor that might even make your eyes water. Usually, molds, yeasts, or an off color accompany truly putrid-smelling sauerkraut.

Reduce strong odors. Normal odors of fermentation occur during the first few days, when the various acids are finding their way out of your jar. After that, odors will be less noticeable.

- Keep a dish of baking soda next to your fermenting sauerkraut, where it will absorb some of the odors.
- Move your ferment to another room in the house, or even the garage, where it is out of the way or better ventilated.
- Invest in water-sealed fermentation lids or a water-sealed fermentation crock, which tend to trap most of the offensive odors. Visit my Shop page at this shortened URL: **fmeasy.me/lids**

INVADERS: FRUIT FLIES AND MAGGOTS

If you are fermenting in an open crock or not able to put a lid on your jar of fermenting sauerkraut, both flies and fruit flies can find it and lay their eggs on the surface. The result? The rather unpleasant discovery of maggots crawling out a few days later.

SET UP A FEW FRUIT-FLY TRAPS

Though most prevalent during warmer months, fruit flies can be a problem all year round. They are attracted to ripening fruit, fermented fruits, tomatoes, melons, squash, bananas, potatoes, and onions. If I notice fruit flies, I set a few fruit-fly traps around my kitchen. I have two effective methods:

Apple cider vinegar bait. Pour a few ounces of apple cider vinegar into a shallow bowl. Plain vinegar does not work. Add a drop or two of dishwasing liquid. The vinegar attracts the flies and the soap reduces surface tension, causing them to drown.

Fruit trap. Place apple cores or other fruit bits in a small bowl and tightly cover with plastic wrap. Use a toothpick to poke a set of holes in the plastic. The fruit attracts the flies and they find their way into the bowl through the tiny holes, but they can't find their way back out. If you're feeling kind, you can take the trap outdoors to release them.

PROTECT YOUR FERMENT

In the summer months when flies are most plentiful, it is imperative that you use a lid to protect your ferment.

REMOVE THE INFESTED LAYER

If you do find maggots in your crock of sauerkraut, there is no need to panic or discard the whole batch.

> *As they hatch on the surface of a ferment, maggots migrate up and out of the food; they do not burrow farther down. Remove the top inch or so of the fermenting vegetables, and go as deep as necessary until you reach sauerkraut with no signs of maggots, no discoloration, and a pleasant aroma. Be sure to wipe the interior sides of the vessel to remove any lingering maggots or eggs.*
>
> —Sandor Katz, *The Art of Fermentation*

PART 4

A Palette of Sauerkraut Recipes to Please Any Palate

You are about to have your taste buds tantalized by a wide range of flavorful sauerkraut recipes. Who knew you could add pineapple to a sauerkraut recipe? Whether you are craving a bit of sweetness, spicy heat, or just something plain and simple, there's a recipe for you.

If this is your first time making sauerkraut, first go to Chapter 8: Small-Batch Fermentation Teaching Recipe. It contains valuable tips, numerous photos, and additional notes not included in the recipes found in this section.

FREE BOOK BONUS

Free DOWNLOAD

To download a Visual Ingredients Guide for all the recipes in this book, visit this shortened URL: **fmeasy.me/mwsk**

For each of the recipes you will need the following equipment (Described in detail in chapter 7, p.31):

- Kitchen scale, ideally digital
- 1-quart (1 L) wide-mouth canning jar, or similar sized jar
- 4-ounce (125 ml) canning jar (jelly jar), or fermentation weight of choice
- Wide-mouth plastic storage cap, or canning jar lid and rim, or air lock lid of choice
- Cutting board and chef's knife
- Large mixing bowl
- Vegetable peeler, measuring spoons, and grater
- Kraut pounder (optional)

SAUERKRAUT FUN FACT

During World War I, due to concerns that the American public would reject a product with a German name, American sauerkraut makers relabeled their product "liberty cabbage."

CHAPTER 10

Simple Sauerkraut Recipes

BARE-NAKED SAUERKRAUT, (P.70)

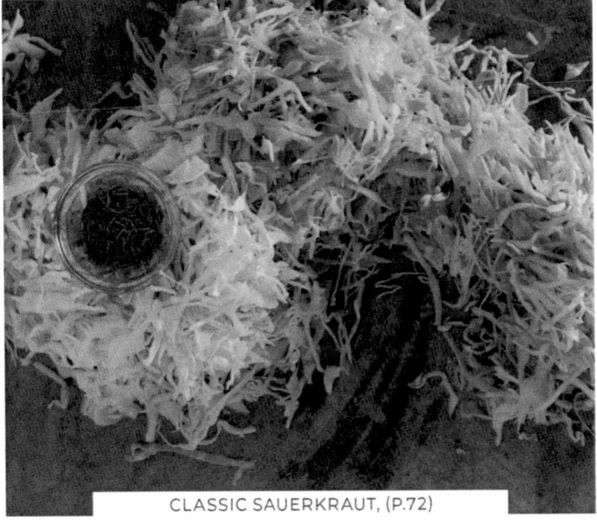
CLASSIC SAUERKRAUT, (P.72)

DILLY DELIGHT SAUERKRAUT, (P.74)

LEMON DILL-LIGHT SAUERKRAUT, (P.76)

Bare-Naked Sauerkraut—Just Cabbage

When life gives you cabbage, you make sauerkraut. For those of you who want to keep life simple, this is your recipe. Shred cabbage, mix in salt, and pack the juicy mass—along with all those hardworking bacteria—into a jar. Easy peasy.

Bare-Naked Sauerkraut, crunchy and delightfully sour, makes a perfect accompaniment to any dish.

MAKES 1 QUART (1 L) OF SAUERKRAUT TEEMING WITH TRILLIONS OF BENEFICIAL BACTERIA.

FERMENTATION TIME: 2–4 WEEKS

INGREDIENTS

1 medium head fresh green cabbage, 2–3 pounds (1 kg)

1 tablespoon (15 ml) fine-grain iodine-free salt

INSTRUCTIONS

1 **SET UP.** Place your bowl on the scale. Either zero out the scale or write down the tare of your bowl.

2 **CHOP.** Set aside a clean cabbage leaf for use in step 5. Quarter the cabbage, leaving the core in, and slice into thin strips until close to core, tossing the core. Add sliced cabbage to your bowl until the weight of the vegetables and cabbage is 1¾ pounds (28 oz or 800 g).

3 **SALT.** Sprinkle with 1 tablespoon salt—that's 16 grams (or 2%) by weight. Thoroughly mix until salt is well dispersed. Let sit at room temperature for 20 minutes to allow the salt to pull the water out of the vegetables. Then massage the cabbage with strong hands until it clumps together and a puddle of brine can be seen when tipping bowl to the side.

4 **PACK.** Pack mixture into your jar, pressing cabbage down tightly with your fist to allow the brine to rise. Leave 1½–2 inches (4–5 cm) of space between the top of your cabbage and the top of the jar.

5 **SUBMERGE AND SEAL.** Take the cabbage leaf saved in step 2, tear it to just fit inside the jar, and place it on top of the packed mixture. Using your preferred weight to hold the mixture below the brine, screw on lid or air lock lid of choice, following product directions. Label your jar with date and flavor.

6 **FERMENT.** Let ferment for 2–4 weeks. Place in a shallow bowl on your kitchen counter, out of direct sunlight—ideally between 65 and 72 °F (18–22 °C)—to ferment until texture and tang is to your liking.

7 **STORE.** Open the jar, remove the weight, and clean rim and jar. Firmly screw on storage lid. Add fermentation time to your label and place in your refrigerator.

Consider fermenting vegetables as a group activity. Enlist the kids, your significant other, friends, and guest to chop, slice, or grate, salt, and massage, pound, or press vegetables into a crock. No experience is necessary, so even the youngest member can participate. And for the "I don't like kraut" set, they're sure to at least taste the ferment they helped make.

—Kirsten K. Shockey and Christopher Shockey, *Fermented Vegetables*

Enjoy!

Classic Sauerkraut—With a Traditional Sauerkraut Spice

You'll see many traditional recipes for sauerkraut calling for the addition of caraway seeds. They impart a warm, earthy flavor with a slight hint of licorice.

MAKES 1 QUART (1 L) OF SAUERKRAUT TEEMING WITH TRILLIONS OF BENEFICIAL BACTERIA.
FERMENTATION TIME: 2–4 WEEKS

INGREDIENTS

1 teaspoon (5 ml) caraway seeds

1 medium head fresh green cabbage, 2–3 pounds (1 kg)

1 tablespoon (15 ml) fine-grain iodine-free salt

INSTRUCTIONS

1 **SET UP.** Place your bowl on the scale. Either zero out the scale or write down the tare of your bowl.

2 **CHOP.** Sprinkle caraway seeds into your bowl. Set aside a clean cabbage leaf for use in step 5. Quarter the cabbage, leaving the core in, and slice into thin strips until close to core, tossing the core. Add sliced cabbage to your bowl until the weight of the vegetables and cabbage is 1¾ pounds (28 oz or 800 g).

3 **SALT.** Sprinkle with 1 tablespoon salt—that's 16 grams (or 2%) by weight. Thoroughly mix until salt is well dispersed. Let sit at room temperature for 20 minutes to allow the salt to pull the water out of the vegetables. Then massage the cabbage with strong hands until it clumps together and a puddle of brine can be seen when tipping bowl to the side.

4 **PACK.** Pack mixture into your jar, pressing cabbage down tightly with your fist to allow the brine to rise. Leave 1½–2 inches (4–5 cm) of space between the top of your cabbage and the top of the jar.

5 **SUBMERGE AND SEAL.** Take the cabbage leaf saved in step 2, tear it to just fit inside the jar, and place it on top of the packed mixture. Using your preferred weight to hold the mixture below the brine, screw on lid or air lock lid of choice, following product directions. Label your jar with date and flavor.

6 **FERMENT.** Let ferment for 2–4 weeks. Place in a shallow bowl on your kitchen counter, out of direct sunlight—ideally between 65 and 72 °F (18–22 °C)—to ferment until texture and tang is to your liking.

7 **STORE.** Open the jar, remove the weight, and clean rim and jar. Firmly screw on storage lid. Add fermentation time to your label and place in your refrigerator.

Modern food-processing technologies disconnect us from our food source by separating us from the raw ingredients, keeping us ignorant of what actually happens to them, and ensuring that there is as little human contact with food as possible.

—Jessica Prentice, *Full Moon Feast: Food and the Hunger for Connection*

Enjoy!

Dilly Delight Sauerkraut—Simple

If fish is on the menu, Dilly Delight Sauerkraut should be on the menu, too. This sauerkraut also goes well with lamb.

I love the simplicity of this recipe and tend to use dried dill. Nothing extra to chop.

MAKES 1 QUART (1 L) OF SAUERKRAUT TEEMING WITH TRILLIONS OF BENEFICIAL BACTERIA.

FERMENTATION TIME: 2–4 WEEKS

INGREDIENTS

1 tablespoon (15 ml) dried dill, or 2–3 tablespoons (30–45 ml) fresh

1 medium head fresh green cabbage, 2–3 pounds (1 kg)

1 tablespoon (15 ml) fine-grain iodine-free salt

INSTRUCTIONS

1 **SET UP.** Place your bowl on the scale. Either zero out the scale or write down the tare of your bowl.

2 **CHOP.** Sprinkle dried dill into your bowl. Now, how simple is that? Set aside a clean cabbage leaf for use in step 5. Quarter the cabbage, leaving the core in, and slice into thin strips until close to core, tossing the core. Add sliced cabbage to your bowl until the weight of the vegetables and cabbage is 1¾ pounds (28 oz or 800 g).

3 **SALT.** Sprinkle with 1 tablespoon salt—that's 16 grams (or 2%) by weight. Thoroughly mix until salt is well dispersed. Let sit at room temperature for 20 minutes to allow the salt to pull the water out of the vegetables. Then massage the cabbage with strong hands until it clumps together and a puddle of brine can be seen when tipping bowl to the side.

4 **PACK.** Pack mixture into your jar, pressing cabbage down tightly with your fist to allow the brine to rise. Leave 1½–2 inches (4–5 cm) of space between the top of your cabbage and the top of the jar.

5 **SUBMERGE AND SEAL.** Take the cabbage leaf saved in step 2, tear it to just fit inside the jar, and place it on top of the packed mixture. Using your preferred weight to hold the mixture below the brine, screw on lid or air lock lid of choice, following product directions. Label your jar with date and flavor.

6 **FERMENT.** Let ferment for 2–4 weeks. Place in a shallow bowl on your kitchen counter, out of direct sunlight—ideally between 65 and 72 °F (18–22 °C)—to ferment until texture and tang is to your liking.

7 **STORE.** Open the jar, remove the weight, and clean rim and jar. Firmly screw on storage lid. Add fermentation time to your label and place in your refrigerator.

Your health is your most important asset. Eating well is something you can do every single day to protect yourself and your most important commodity. Adding fermented foods to your daily diet is an essential piece of the clean-eating puzzle, and you can do it easily in any kitchen with nearly any food. Grab a jar and get fermented!

—Jill Ciciarelli, *Fermented, a Four-Season Approach to Paleo Probiotic Foods*

Enjoy!

Lemon Dill-light Sauerkraut—Add Some Sunshine to Your Day

Lemon Dill-light Sauerkraut pairs perfectly with fish. Add some chopped, fresh cilantro and a squeeze of lemon and you're set for a palate-pleasing meal.
Game for a refreshing tzatziki sauce? In your blender, finely chop ½ cup of Lemon Dill-light Sauerkraut. Then, stir into some yogurt along with some fresh mint and diced cucumbers.

MAKES 1 QUART (1 L) OF SAUERKRAUT TEEMING WITH TRILLIONS OF BENEFICIAL BACTERIA.

FERMENTATION TIME: 2–4 WEEKS

INGREDIENTS

1 tablespoon (15 ml) dried dill, or 2–3 tablespoons (30–45 ml) fresh

1 lemon, zest and juice of

1 medium head fresh green cabbage, 2–3 pounds (1 kg)

1 tablespoon (15 ml) fine-grain iodine-free salt

INSTRUCTIONS

1 **SET UP.** Place your bowl on the scale. Either zero out the scale or write down the tare of your bowl.

2 **CHOP.** Prep your lemon zest and add to your bowl along with the dill and lemon juice. Set aside a clean cabbage leaf for use in step 5. Quarter the cabbage, leaving the core in, and slice into thin strips until close to core, tossing the core. Add sliced cabbage to your bowl until the weight of the vegetables and cabbage is 1¾ pounds (28 oz or 800 g).

3 **SALT.** Sprinkle with 1 tablespoon salt—that's 16 grams (or 2%) by weight. Thoroughly mix until salt is well dispersed. Let sit at room temperature for 20 minutes to allow the salt to pull the water out of the vegetables. Then massage the cabbage with strong hands until it clumps together and a puddle of brine can be seen when tipping bowl to the side.

4 **PACK.** Pack mixture into your jar, pressing cabbage down tightly with your fist to allow the brine to rise. Leave 1½–2 inches (4–5 cm) of space between the top of your cabbage and the top of the jar.

5 **SUBMERGE AND SEAL.** Take the cabbage leaf saved in step 2, tear it to just fit inside the jar, and place it on top of the packed mixture. Using your preferred weight to hold the mixture below the brine, screw on lid or air lock lid of choice, following product directions. Label your jar with date and flavor.

6 **FERMENT.** Let ferment for 2–4 weeks. Place in a shallow bowl on your kitchen counter, out of direct sunlight—ideally between 65 and 72 °F (18–22 °C)—to ferment until texture and tang is to your liking.

7 **STORE.** Open the jar, remove the weight, and clean rim and jar. Firmly screw on storage lid. Add fermentation time to your label and place in your refrigerator.

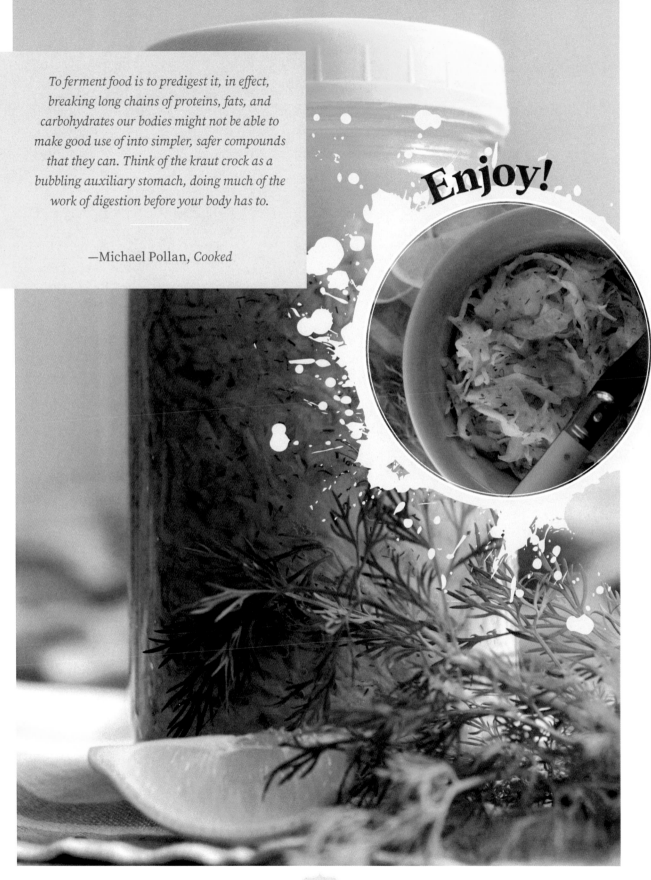

To ferment food is to predigest it, in effect, breaking long chains of proteins, fats, and carbohydrates our bodies might not be able to make good use of into simpler, safer compounds that they can. Think of the kraut crock as a bubbling auxiliary stomach, doing much of the work of digestion before your body has to.

—Michael Pollan, *Cooked*

Enjoy!

CHAPTER 11

Savory Sauerkraut Recipes

THYME FOR LEEKS SAUERKRAUT, (P.80)

JUNIPER BERRY SAUERKRAUT, (P.82)

MEDITERRANEAN BREEZE SAUERKRAUT, (P.84)

Thyme for Leeks Sauerkraut—Savory and Irresistible

Be sure to pull out Thyme for Leeks Sauerkraut when serving your next meal of roast chicken or turkey. It also pairs well with cheese. For an easy appetizer, top a cracker with cheddar cheese and a dollop of Thyme for Leeks Sauerkraut.

A TIP FROM THE SAUERKRAUT WIZARD

For a more tender ferment, select smaller-sized leeks. To remove the bits of dirt and grit that can hide in the layers of the leeks, first slice them lengthwise, then cut into half circles and rinse well.

MAKES 1 QUART (1 L) OF SAUERKRAUT TEEMING WITH TRILLIONS OF BENEFICIAL BACTERIA.

FERMENTATION TIME: 2–4 WEEKS

INGREDIENTS

2 leeks, grit removed, thinly sliced

2–3 carrots, peeled and grated

2–3 garlic cloves, finely minced

1 teaspoon (5 ml) dried thyme, or 1 tablespoon fresh

1 teaspoon (5 ml) dried sage, or 1 tablespoon fresh

1 medium head fresh green cabbage, 2–3 pounds (1 kg)

1 tablespoon (15 ml) fine-grain iodine-free salt

INSTRUCTIONS

1 **SET UP.** Place your bowl on the scale. Either zero out the scale or write down the tare of your bowl.

2 **CHOP.** Prep your leeks, carrots, and garlic and add them to your bowl along with the thyme and sage. Set aside a clean cabbage leaf for use in step 5. Quarter the cabbage, leaving the core in, and slice into thin strips until close to core, tossing the core. Add sliced cabbage to your bowl until the weight of the vegetables and cabbage is 1¾ pounds (28 oz or 800 g).

3 **SALT.** Sprinkle with 1 tablespoon salt—that's 16 grams (or 2%) by weight. Thoroughly mix until salt is well dispersed. Let sit at room temperature for 20 minutes to allow the salt to pull the water out of the vegetables. Then massage the cabbage with strong hands until it clumps together and a puddle of brine can be seen when tipping bowl to the side.

4 **PACK.** Pack mixture into your jar, pressing cabbage down tightly with your fist to allow the brine to rise. Leave 1½–2 inches (4–5 cm) of space between the top of your cabbage and the top of the jar.

5 **SUBMERGE AND SEAL.** Take the cabbage leaf saved in step 2, tear it to just fit inside the jar, and place it on top of the packed mixture. Using your preferred weight to hold the mixture below the brine, screw on lid or air lock lid of choice, following product directions. Label your jar with date and flavor.

6 **FERMENT.** Let ferment for 2–4 weeks. Place in a shallow bowl on your kitchen counter, out of direct sunlight—ideally between 65 and 72 °F (18–22 °C)—to ferment until texture and tang is to your liking.

7 **STORE.** Open the jar, remove the weight, and clean rim and jar. Firmly screw on storage lid. Add fermentation time to your label and place in your refrigerator.

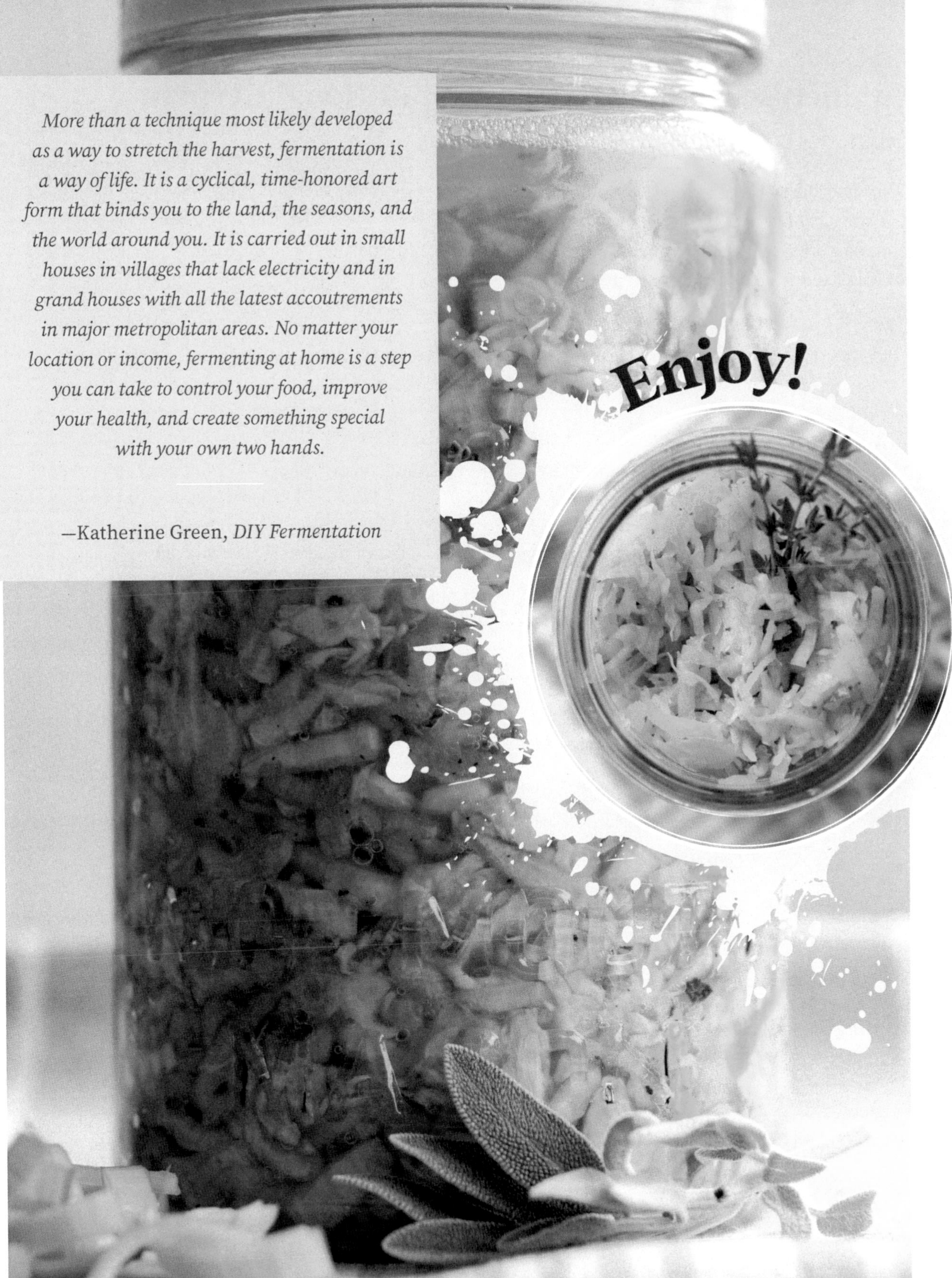

More than a technique most likely developed as a way to stretch the harvest, fermentation is a way of life. It is a cyclical, time-honored art form that binds you to the land, the seasons, and the world around you. It is carried out in small houses in villages that lack electricity and in grand houses with all the latest accoutrements in major metropolitan areas. No matter your location or income, fermenting at home is a step you can take to control your food, improve your health, and create something special with your own two hands.

—Katherine Green, *DIY Fermentation*

Juniper Berry Sauerkraut—A Traditional German Sauerkraut Spice

A juniper berry is the female seed cone produced by the various species of junipers, and is used in making gin. It adds a piney, woodsy flavor to your ferment.

A roast pork dinner is not complete without a serving of Juniper Berry Sauerkraut. It is also great added to your favorite potato salad recipe.

A TIP FROM THE SAUERKRAUT WIZARD

Don't just go out and grab the berries off the juniper tree in your backyard; some are considered too bitter to eat. You should find juniper berries at your local health food store or at a well-stocked commercial grocery store.

A TIP FROM THE SAUERKRAUT WIZARD

When using rosemary, remove the needles from the stalks and discard the stalks. Store rosemary wrapped in a damp paper towel and keep in your refrigerator.

MAKES 1 QUART (1 L) OF SAUERKRAUT TEEMING WITH TRILLIONS OF BENEFICIAL BACTERIA.

FERMENTATION TIME: 2–4 WEEKS

INGREDIENTS

½ medium onion, thinly sliced

2–3 garlic cloves, finely minced

1 tablespoon (15 ml) juniper berries, lightly crushed

1 tablespoon (15 ml) fresh rosemary, roughly chopped

1 medium head fresh green cabbage, 2–3 pounds (1 kg)

1 tablespoon (15 ml) fine-grain iodine-free salt

INSTRUCTIONS

1 **SET UP.** Place your bowl on the scale. Either zero out the scale or write down the tare of your bowl.

2 **CHOP.** Prep your onion, garlic, and rosemary and add to your bowl along with the juniper berries. Set aside a clean cabbage leaf for use in step 5. Quarter the cabbage, leaving the core in, and slice into thin strips until close to core, tossing the core. Add sliced cabbage to your bowl until the weight of the vegetables and cabbage is 1¾ pounds (28 oz or 800 g).

3 **SALT.** Sprinkle with 1 tablespoon salt—that's 16 grams (or 2%) by weight. Thoroughly mix until salt is well dispersed. Let sit at room temperature for 20 minutes to allow the salt to pull the water out of the vegetables. Then massage the cabbage with strong hands until it clumps together and a puddle of brine can be seen when tipping bowl to the side.

4 **PACK.** Pack mixture into your jar, pressing cabbage down tightly with your fist to allow the brine to rise. Leave 1½–2 inches (4–5 cm) of space between the top of your cabbage and the top of the jar.

5 **SUBMERGE AND SEAL.** Take the cabbage leaf saved in step 2, tear it to just fit inside the jar, and place it on top of the packed mixture. Using your preferred weight to hold the mixture below the brine, screw on lid or air lock lid of choice, following product directions. Label your jar with date and flavor.

6 **FERMENT.** Let ferment for 2–4 weeks. Place in a shallow bowl on your kitchen counter, out of direct sunlight—ideally between 65 and 72 °F (18–22 °C)—to ferment until texture and tang is to your liking.

7 **STORE.** Open the jar, remove the weight, and clean rim and jar. Firmly screw on storage lid. Add fermentation time to your label and place in your refrigerator.

> *Your role as a "fermenter" is to facilitate this seemingly magic process by creating the most favourable conditions possible for the micro-organisms you wish to employ to preserve and enhance your chosen foodstuffs, while guarding against infiltration by putrefying bacteria, which would otherwise cause the food to spoil.*
>
> —Holly Davis, *Ferment*

Enjoy!

Mediterranean Breeze Sauerkraut—Spices from Morocco ... with Love

Mediterranean Breeze Sauerkraut goes well with lamb or Greek cuisine. Try stirring some of this sauerkraut into couscous. Top with chopped dates, pine nuts, and yogurt.

MAKES 1 QUART (1 L) OF SAUERKRAUT TEEMING WITH TRILLIONS OF BENEFICIAL BACTERIA.

FERMENTATION TIME: 2–4 WEEKS

INGREDIENTS

2–3 carrots, peeled and grated

2–3 garlic cloves, finely minced

½ medium onion, thinly sliced

½ cup (120 ml) fresh cilantro, coarsely chopped

1 lemon, zest and juice of

1 teaspoon (5 ml) ground cinnamon

1 teaspoon (5 ml) coriander powder

1 teaspoon (5 ml) cumin seeds

1 medium head fresh green cabbage, 2–3 pounds (1 kg)

1 tablespoon (15 ml) fine-grain iodine-free salt

INSTRUCTIONS

1 **SET UP.** Place your bowl on the scale. Either zero out the scale or write down the tare of your bowl.

2 **CHOP.** Prep your carrots, garlic, onions, lemon zest, and cilantro and add them to your bowl along with the cinnamon, coriander, cumin, and lemon juice. Set aside a clean cabbage leaf for use in step 5. Quarter the cabbage, leaving the core in, and slice into thin strips until close to core, tossing the core. Add sliced cabbage to your bowl until the weight of the vegetables and cabbage is 1¾ pounds (28 oz or 800 g).

3 **SALT.** Sprinkle with 1 tablespoon salt—that's 16 grams (or 2%) by weight. Thoroughly mix until salt is well dispersed. Let sit at room temperature for 20 minutes to allow the salt to pull the water out of the vegetables. Then massage the cabbage with strong hands until it clumps together and a puddle of brine can be seen when tipping bowl to the side.

4 **PACK.** Pack mixture into your jar, pressing cabbage down tightly with your fist to allow the brine to rise. Leave 1½–2 inches (4–5 cm) of space between the top of your cabbage and the top of the jar.

5 **SUBMERGE AND SEAL.** Take the cabbage leaf saved in step 2, tear it to just fit inside the jar, and place it on top of the packed mixture. Using your preferred weight to hold the mixture below the brine, screw on lid or air lock lid of choice, following product directions. Label your jar with date and flavor.

6 **FERMENT.** Let ferment for 2–4 weeks. Place in a shallow bowl on your kitchen counter, out of direct sunlight—ideally between 65 and 72 °F (18–22 °C)—to ferment until texture and tang is to your liking.

7 **STORE.** Open the jar, remove the weight, and clean rim and jar. Firmly screw on storage lid. Add fermentation time to your label and place in your refrigerator.

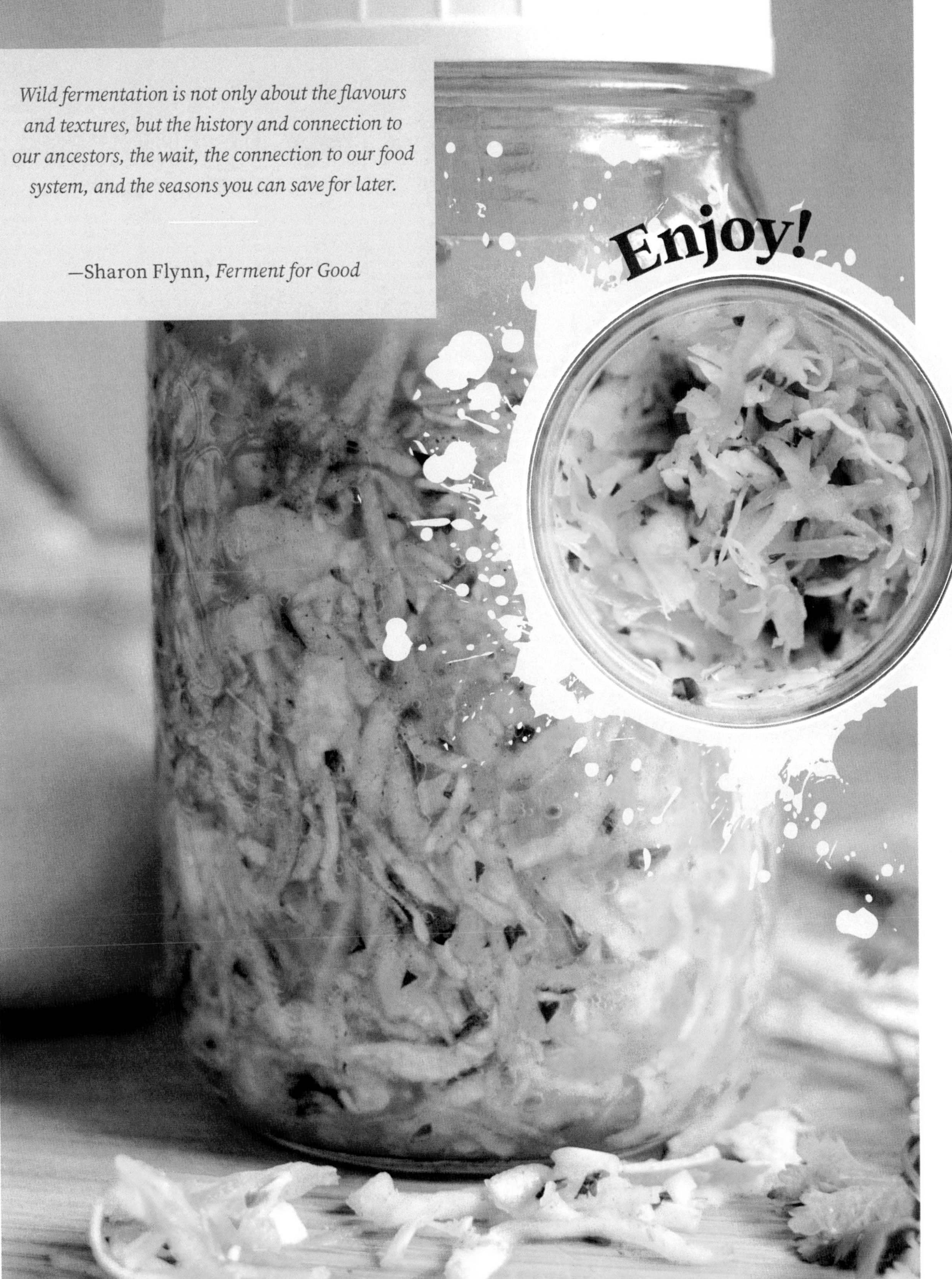

Wild fermentation is not only about the flavours and textures, but the history and connection to our ancestors, the wait, the connection to our food system, and the seasons you can save for later.

—Sharon Flynn, *Ferment for Good*

CHAPTER 12

Sauerkraut Recipes Powered by Beets

PASSION PINK SAUERKRAUT, (P.88)

RUBY-RED RED-CABBAGE SAUERKRAUT (P.90)

CARDAMOM BEET SAUERKRAUT, (P.92)

ROSEMARY BEET SAUERKRAUT, (P.94)

Passion Pink Sauerkraut—A Love of Beets

The beets in Passion Pink Sauerkraut turn this ferment a vibrant pink. Beets are an amazing source of minerals and unique health-boosting nutrients. These grungy-looking roots are sweet, impart a beautiful ruby-red color to your sauerkraut, and pack tons of flavor underneath their rugged exterior. In addition, they are a wonderful tonic for the liver, working to purify the blood.

Use Passion Pink Sauerkraut to make a quick salad: lettuce, crumbled blue cheese, some nuts, olive oil, and a splash of balsamic vinegar.

A TIP FROM THE SAUERKRAUT WIZARD

Beets can be tough to grate. Peel them first to get rid of the "dirt" taste, and if you're making an extra-large batch of sauerkraut, use your food processor.

MAKES 1 QUART (1 L) OF SAUERKRAUT TEEMING WITH TRILLIONS OF BENEFICIAL BACTERIA.

FERMENTATION TIME: 2–4 WEEKS

INGREDIENTS

1–2 medium beets (baseball size), peeled and grated

2–3 garlic cloves, finely minced

1 teaspoon (5 ml) caraway seeds

1 medium head fresh green cabbage, 2–3 pounds (1 kg)

1 tablespoon (15 ml) fine-grain iodine-free salt

INSTRUCTIONS

1 **SET UP.** Place your bowl on the scale. Either zero out the scale or write down the tare of your bowl.

2 **CHOP.** Prep your beets and garlic and add to your bowl along with the caraway seeds. Set aside a clean cabbage leaf for use in step 5. Quarter the cabbage, leaving the core in, and slice into thin strips until close to core, tossing the core. Add sliced cabbage to your bowl until the weight of the vegetables and cabbage is 1¾ pounds (28 oz or 800 g).

3 **SALT.** Sprinkle with 1 tablespoon salt—that's 16 grams (or 2%) by weight. Thoroughly mix until salt is well dispersed. Let sit at room temperature for 20 minutes to allow the salt to pull the water out of the vegetables. Then massage the cabbage with strong hands until it clumps together and a puddle of brine can be seen when tipping bowl to the side.

4 **PACK.** Pack mixture into your jar, pressing cabbage down tightly with your fist to allow the brine to rise. Leave 1½–2 inches (4–5 cm) of space between the top of your cabbage and the top of the jar.

5 **SUBMERGE AND SEAL.** Take the cabbage leaf saved in step 2, tear it to just fit inside the jar, and place it on top of the packed mixture. Using your preferred weight to hold the mixture below the brine, screw on lid or air lock lid of choice, following product directions. Label your jar with date and flavor.

6 **FERMENT.** Let ferment for 2–4 weeks. Place in a shallow bowl on your kitchen counter, out of direct sunlight—ideally between 65 and 72 °F (18–22 °C)—to ferment until texture and tang is to your liking.

7 **STORE.** Open the jar, remove the weight, and clean rim and jar. Firmly screw on storage lid. Add fermentation time to your label and place in your refrigerator.

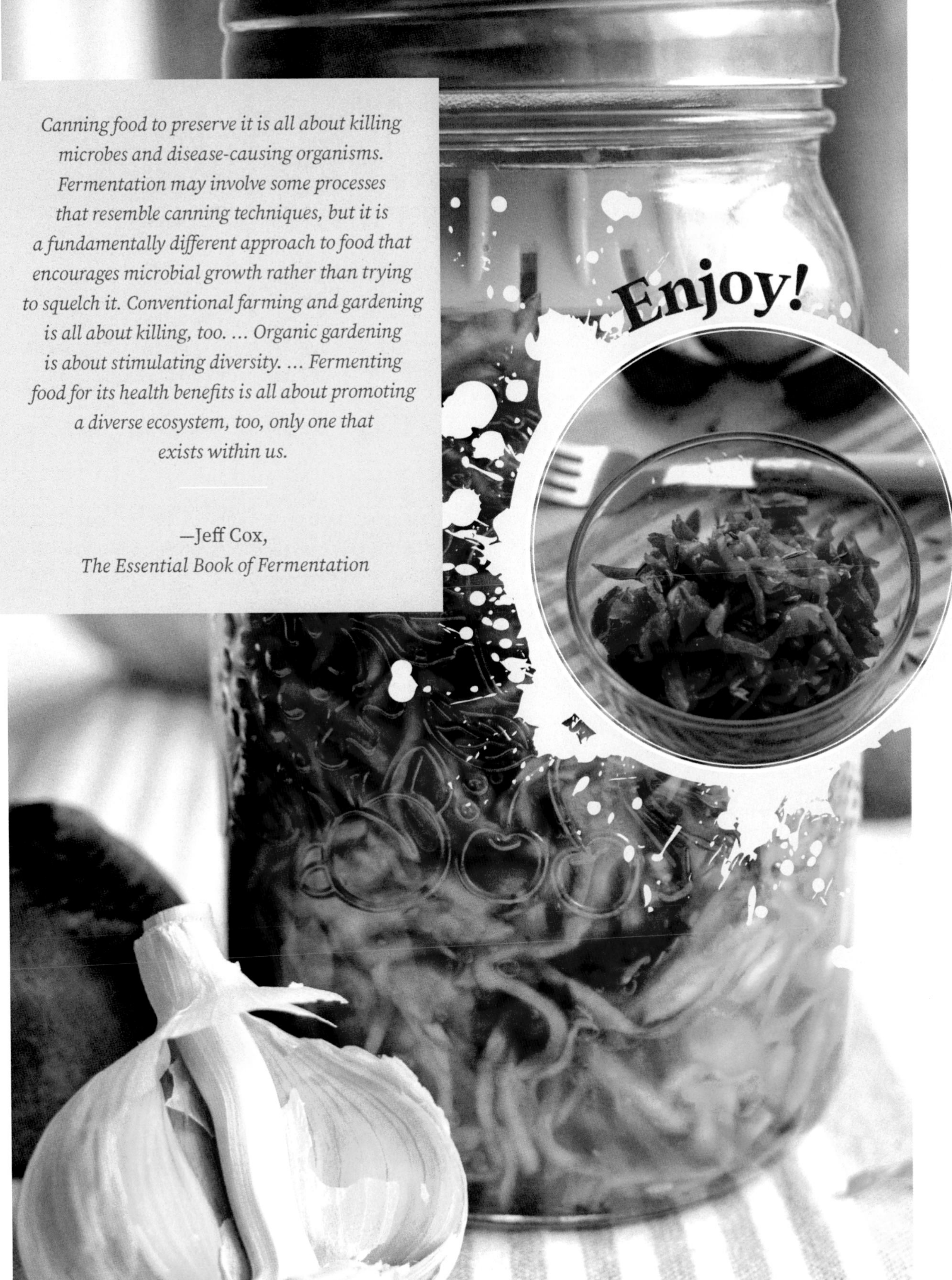

Canning food to preserve it is all about killing microbes and disease-causing organisms. Fermentation may involve some processes that resemble canning techniques, but it is a fundamentally different approach to food that encourages microbial growth rather than trying to squelch it. Conventional farming and gardening is all about killing, too. ... Organic gardening is about stimulating diversity. ... Fermenting food for its health benefits is all about promoting a diverse ecosystem, too, only one that exists within us.

—Jeff Cox,
The Essential Book of Fermentation

Ruby-Red Red-Cabbage Sauerkraut

There are many nutritional benefits hidden in red-cabbage sauerkraut. Just like in pigment-rich blueberries, the compounds that give red cabbage its distinctive dark color act as antioxidants. Red cabbage has one of the highest levels of naturally available vitamin C, more even than oranges. And of course, this sauerkraut is rich in various strains of beneficial bacteria.
Probiotics + antioxidants + vitamin C make this sauerkraut a triple winner.

A TIP FROM THE SAUERKRAUT WIZARD

When I add fruit to a ferment, I shorten the fermentation time. The extra sugar from the apple gives the bacteria extra sugar to consume, and if left to ferment for too long, your ferment can shift toward the alcohol side.

MAKES 1 QUART (1 L) OF SAUERKRAUT TEEMING WITH TRILLIONS OF BENEFICIAL BACTERIA.

FERMENTATION TIME: 1–2 WEEKS

INGREDIENTS

1–2 medium beet (baseball size), peeled and grated

1 tart apple, peeled and finely diced

1 2-inch (5 cm) piece of fresh ginger root, peeled and finely grated

1 medium head fresh red cabbage, 2–3 pounds (1 kg)

1 tablespoon (15 ml) fine-grain iodine-free salt

INSTRUCTIONS

1 **SET UP.** Place your bowl on the scale. Either zero out the scale or write down the tare of your bowl.

2 **CHOP.** Prep your beet, apple, and ginger and add to your bowl. Set aside a clean cabbage leaf for use in step 5. Quarter the cabbage, leaving the core in, and slice into thin strips until close to core, tossing the core. Add sliced cabbage to your bowl until the weight of the vegetables and cabbage is 1¾ pounds (28 oz or 800 g).

3 **SALT.** Sprinkle with 1 tablespoon salt—that's 16 grams (or 2%) by weight. Thoroughly mix until salt is well dispersed. Let sit at room temperature for 20 minutes to allow the salt to pull the water out of the vegetables. Then massage the cabbage with strong hands until it clumps together and a puddle of brine can be seen when tipping bowl to the side.

4 **PACK.** Pack mixture into your jar, pressing cabbage down tightly with your fist to allow the brine to rise. Leave 1½–2 inches (4–5 cm) of space between the top of your cabbage and the top of the jar.

5 **SUBMERGE AND SEAL.** Take the cabbage leaf saved in step 2, tear it to just fit inside the jar, and place it on top of the packed mixture. Using your preferred weight to hold the mixture below the brine, screw on lid or air lock lid of choice, following product directions. Label your jar with date and flavor.

6 **FERMENT.** Let ferment for 2–4 weeks. Place in a shallow bowl on your kitchen counter, out of direct sunlight—ideally between 65 and 72 °F (18–22 °C)—to ferment until texture and tang is to your liking.

7 **STORE.** Open the jar, remove the weight, and clean rim and jar. Firmly screw on storage lid. Add fermentation time to your label and place in your refrigerator.

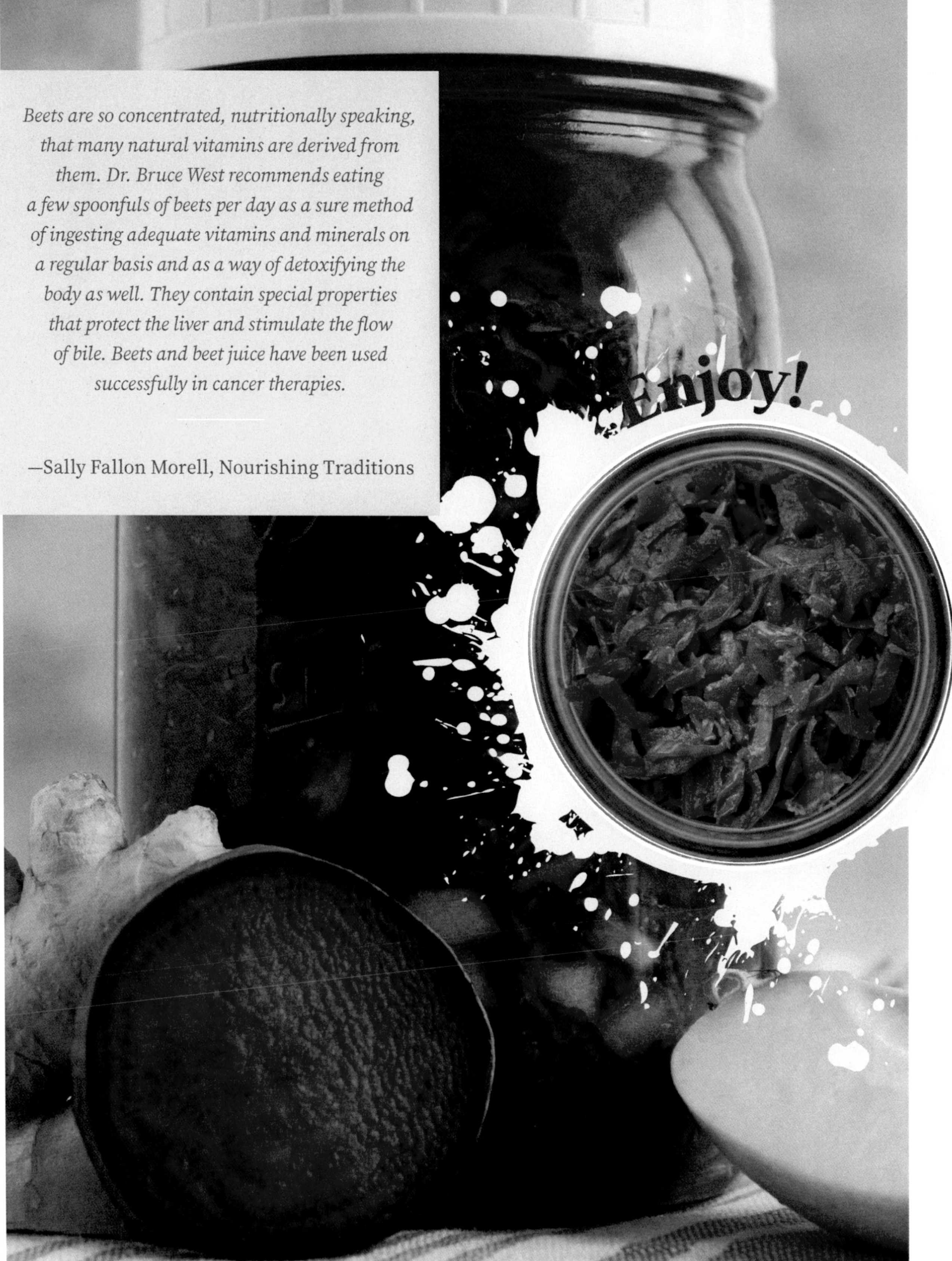

Beets are so concentrated, nutritionally speaking, that many natural vitamins are derived from them. Dr. Bruce West recommends eating a few spoonfuls of beets per day as a sure method of ingesting adequate vitamins and minerals on a regular basis and as a way of detoxifying the body as well. They contain special properties that protect the liver and stimulate the flow of bile. Beets and beet juice have been used successfully in cancer therapies.

—Sally Fallon Morell, Nourishing Traditions

Cardamom Beet Sauerkraut—Earthy, Sweet, and Deeply Nourishing

I love to use my beet-infused sauerkrauts to top my daily salad. Add to lettuce along with some nuts and cheese and top with a drizzle of olive oil.

A TIP FROM THE SAUERKRAUT WIZARD
Old beets that have been stored for months can be tough to grate. Look for fresh beets—with their tops on—and be sure to peel them first to remove any "dirt-like" taste.

MAKES 1 QUART (1 L) OF SAUERKRAUT TEEMING WITH TRILLIONS OF BENEFICIAL BACTERIA.
FERMENTATION TIME: 2–4 WEEKS

INGREDIENTS

1–2 medium beets (baseball size), peeled and grated

1 2-inch (5 cm) piece of fresh ginger root, peeled and finely grated

1 teaspoon (5 ml) dried tarragon

1 teaspoon (5 ml) cardamom powder

½ teaspoon (2 ml) ground cloves

1 medium head fresh green cabbage, 2–3 pounds (1 kg)

1 tablespoon (15 ml) fine-grain iodine-free salt

INSTRUCTIONS

1 **SET UP.** Place your bowl on the scale. Either zero out the scale or write down the tare of your bowl.

2 **CHOP.** Prep your beets and ginger. Add them to your bowl along with the tarragon, cardamom, and cloves. Set aside a clean cabbage leaf for use in step 5. Quarter the cabbage, leaving the core in, and slice into thin strips until close to core, tossing the core. Add sliced cabbage to your bowl until the weight of the vegetables and cabbage is 1¾ pounds (28 oz or 800 g).

3 **SALT.** Sprinkle with 1 tablespoon salt—that's 16 grams (or 2%) by weight. Thoroughly mix until salt is well dispersed. Let sit at room temperature for 20 minutes to allow the salt to pull the water out of the vegetables. Then massage the cabbage with strong hands until it clumps together and a puddle of brine can be seen when tipping bowl to the side.

4 **PACK.** Pack mixture into your jar, pressing cabbage down tightly with your fist to allow the brine to rise. Leave 1½–2 inches (4–5 cm) of space between the top of your cabbage and the top of the jar.

5 **SUBMERGE AND SEAL.** Take the cabbage leaf saved in step 2, tear it to just fit inside the jar, and place it on top of the packed mixture. Using your preferred weight to hold the mixture below the brine, screw on lid or air lock lid of choice, following product directions. Label your jar with date and flavor.

6 **FERMENT.** Let ferment for 2–4 weeks. Place in a shallow bowl on your kitchen counter, out of direct sunlight—ideally between 65 and 72 °F (18–22 °C)—to ferment until texture and tang is to your liking.

7 **STORE.** Open the jar, remove the weight, and clean rim and jar. Firmly screw on storage lid. Add fermentation time to your label and place in your refrigerator.

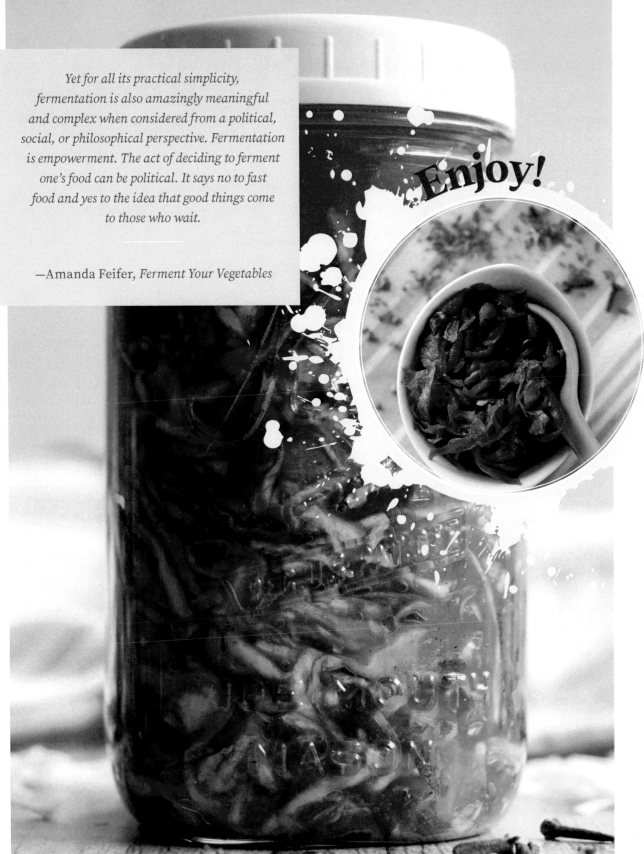

Yet for all its practical simplicity, fermentation is also amazingly meaningful and complex when considered from a political, social, or philosophical perspective. Fermentation is empowerment. The act of deciding to ferment one's food can be political. It says no to fast food and yes to the idea that good things come to those who wait.

—Amanda Feifer, *Ferment Your Vegetables*

Enjoy!

Rosemary Beet Sauerkraut—Sweet and Savory

This recipe includes onions, a natural prebiotic. In your gut, onions—along with carrots, garlic, and leeks—nourish the healthy bacteria already living in your intestines. In a sauerkraut recipe, they kick-start the fermentation process.

> **A TIP FROM THE SAUERKRAUT WIZARD**
> For ease of use, I tend to ferment with dried herbs. For rosemary, however, I do prefer it fresh and will go out of my way to purchase it. If you have to use dried rosemary, you'll need less, typically one-third the amount. Use 1 teaspoon dried rosemary for 1 tablespoon fresh.

MAKES 1 QUART (1 L) OF SAUERKRAUT TEEMING WITH TRILLIONS OF BENEFICIAL BACTERIA.

FERMENTATION TIME: 2–4 WEEKS

INGREDIENTS

1–2 medium beets (baseball size), peeled and grated

½ medium onion, thinly sliced

1 tablespoon (15 ml) fresh rosemary, roughly chopped

1 medium head fresh green cabbage, 2–3 pounds (1 kg)

1 tablespoon (15 ml) fine-grain iodine-free salt

INSTRUCTIONS

1 **SET UP.** Place your bowl on the scale. Either zero out the scale or write down the tare of your bowl.

2 **CHOP.** Prep your beets, onion, and rosemary and add to your bowl. Set aside a clean cabbage leaf for use in step 5. Quarter the cabbage, leaving the core in, and slice into thin strips until close to core, tossing the core. Add sliced cabbage to your bowl until the weight of the vegetables and cabbage is 1¾ pounds (28 oz or 800 g).

3 **SALT.** Sprinkle with 1 tablespoon salt—that's 16 grams (or 2%) by weight. Thoroughly mix until salt is well dispersed. Let sit at room temperature for 20 minutes to allow the salt to pull the water out of the vegetables. Then massage the cabbage with strong hands until it clumps together and a puddle of brine can be seen when tipping bowl to the side.

4 **PACK.** Pack mixture into your jar, pressing cabbage down tightly with your fist to allow the brine to rise. Leave 1½–2 inches (4–5 cm) of space between the top of your cabbage and the top of the jar.

5 **SUBMERGE AND SEAL.** Take the cabbage leaf saved in step 2, tear it to just fit inside the jar, and place it on top of the packed mixture. Using your preferred weight to hold the mixture below the brine, screw on lid or air lock lid of choice, following product directions. Label your jar with date and flavor.

6 **FERMENT.** Let ferment for 2–4 weeks. Place in a shallow bowl on your kitchen counter, out of direct sunlight—ideally between 65 and 72 °F (18–22 °C)—to ferment until texture and tang is to your liking.

7 **STORE.** Open the jar, remove the weight, and clean rim and jar. Firmly screw on storage lid. Add fermentation time to your label and place in your refrigerator.

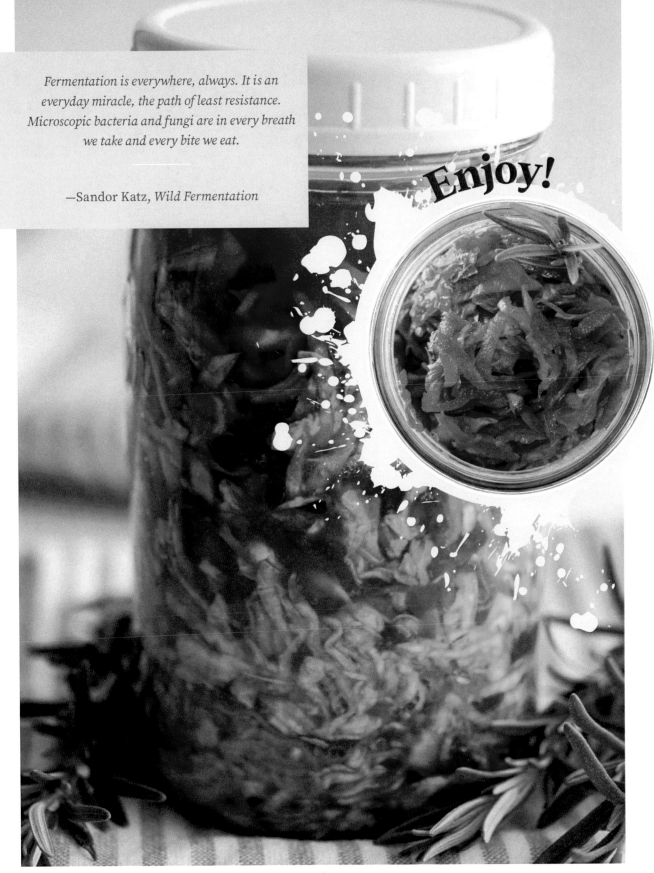

Fermentation is everywhere, always. It is an everyday miracle, the path of least resistance. Microscopic bacteria and fungi are in every breath we take and every bite we eat.

—Sandor Katz, *Wild Fermentation*

Enjoy!

CHAPTER 13

Sauerkraut Recipes with a Touch of Sweetness

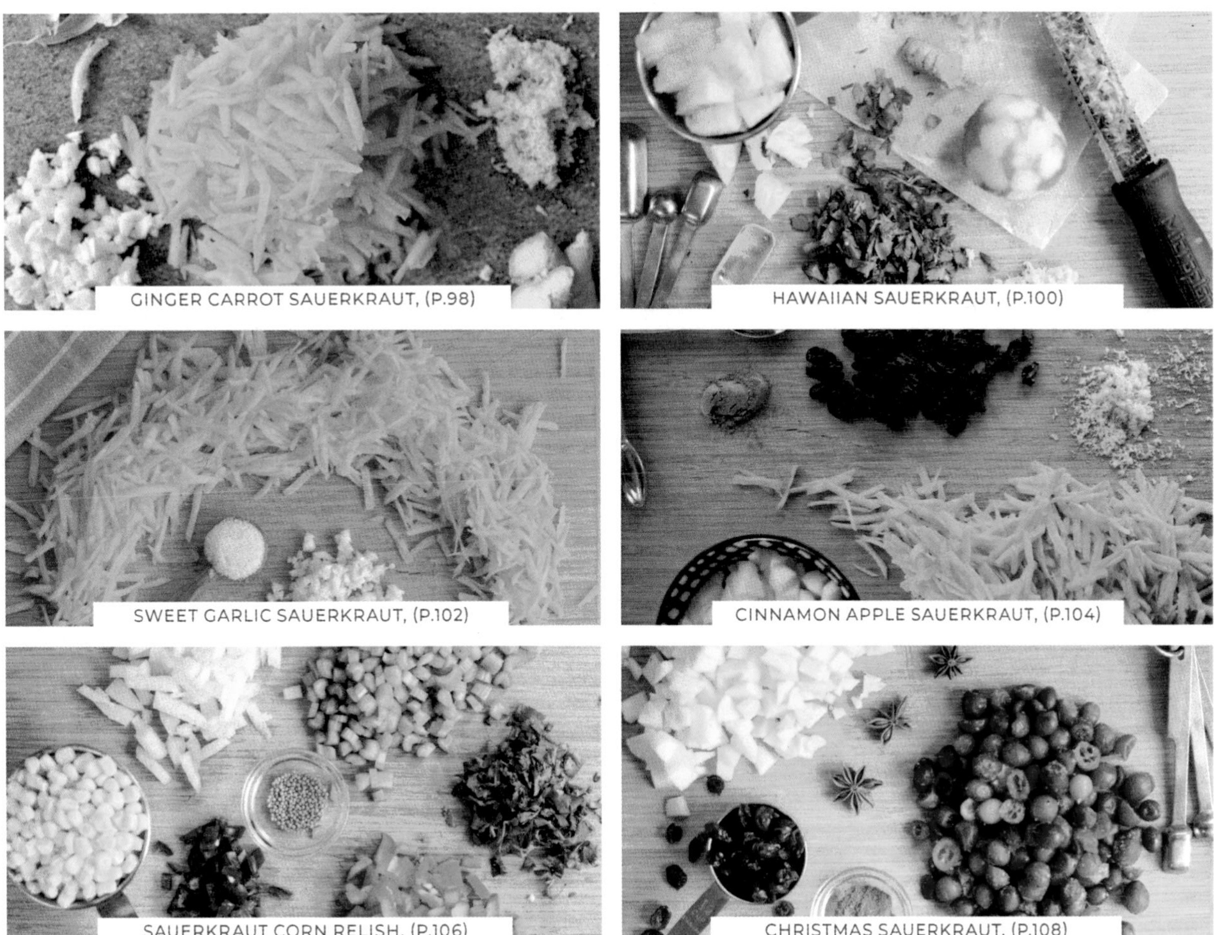

GINGER CARROT SAUERKRAUT, (P.98)

HAWAIIAN SAUERKRAUT, (P.100)

SWEET GARLIC SAUERKRAUT, (P.102)

CINNAMON APPLE SAUERKRAUT, (P.104)

SAUERKRAUT CORN RELISH, (P.106)

CHRISTMAS SAUERKRAUT, (P.108)

Ginger Carrot Sauerkraut—A Mellowed Sweet and Spicy Bite

My family can never get enough of Ginger Carrot Sauerkraut. It is full of sweet carrots and has a touch of spicy ginger to add a nice depth of flavor and help with digestion—along with all those magical microbes living in the sauerkraut.

Enjoy this sauerkraut recipe and experiment with just how much ginger you like.

MAKES 1 QUART (1 L) OF SAUERKRAUT TEEMING WITH TRILLIONS OF BENEFICIAL BACTERIA.

FERMENTATION TIME: 2–4 WEEKS

INGREDIENTS

2–3 carrots, peeled and grated

2–3 garlic cloves, finely minced

1 2-inch (5 cm) piece of fresh ginger root, peeled and finely grated

1 medium head fresh green cabbage, 2–3 pounds (1 kg)

1 tablespoon (15 ml) fine-grain iodine-free salt

INSTRUCTIONS

1. **SET UP.** Place your bowl on the scale. Either zero out the scale or write down the tare of your bowl.

2. **CHOP.** Prep your carrots, garlic, and ginger and add to your bowl. Set aside a clean cabbage leaf for use in step 5. Quarter the cabbage, leaving the core in, and slice into thin strips until close to core, tossing the core. Add sliced cabbage to your bowl until the weight of the vegetables and cabbage is 1¾ pounds (28 oz or 800 g).

3. **SALT.** Sprinkle with 1 tablespoon salt—that's 16 grams (or 2%) by weight. Thoroughly mix until salt is well dispersed. Let sit at room temperature for 20 minutes to allow the salt to pull the water out of the vegetables. Then massage the cabbage with strong hands until it clumps together and a puddle of brine can be seen when tipping bowl to the side.

4. **PACK.** Pack mixture into your jar, pressing cabbage down tightly with your fist to allow the brine to rise. Leave 1½–2 inches (4–5 cm) of space between the top of your cabbage and the top of the jar.

5. **SUBMERGE AND SEAL.** Take the cabbage leaf saved in step 2, tear it to just fit inside the jar, and place it on top of the packed mixture. Using your preferred weight to hold the mixture below the brine, screw on lid or air lock lid of choice, following product directions. Label your jar with date and flavor.

6. **FERMENT.** Let ferment for 2–4 weeks. Place in a shallow bowl on your kitchen counter, out of direct sunlight—ideally between 65 and 72 °F (18–22 °C)—to ferment until texture and tang is to your liking.

7. **STORE.** Open the jar, remove the weight, and clean rim and jar. Firmly screw on storage lid. Add fermentation time to your label and place in your refrigerator.

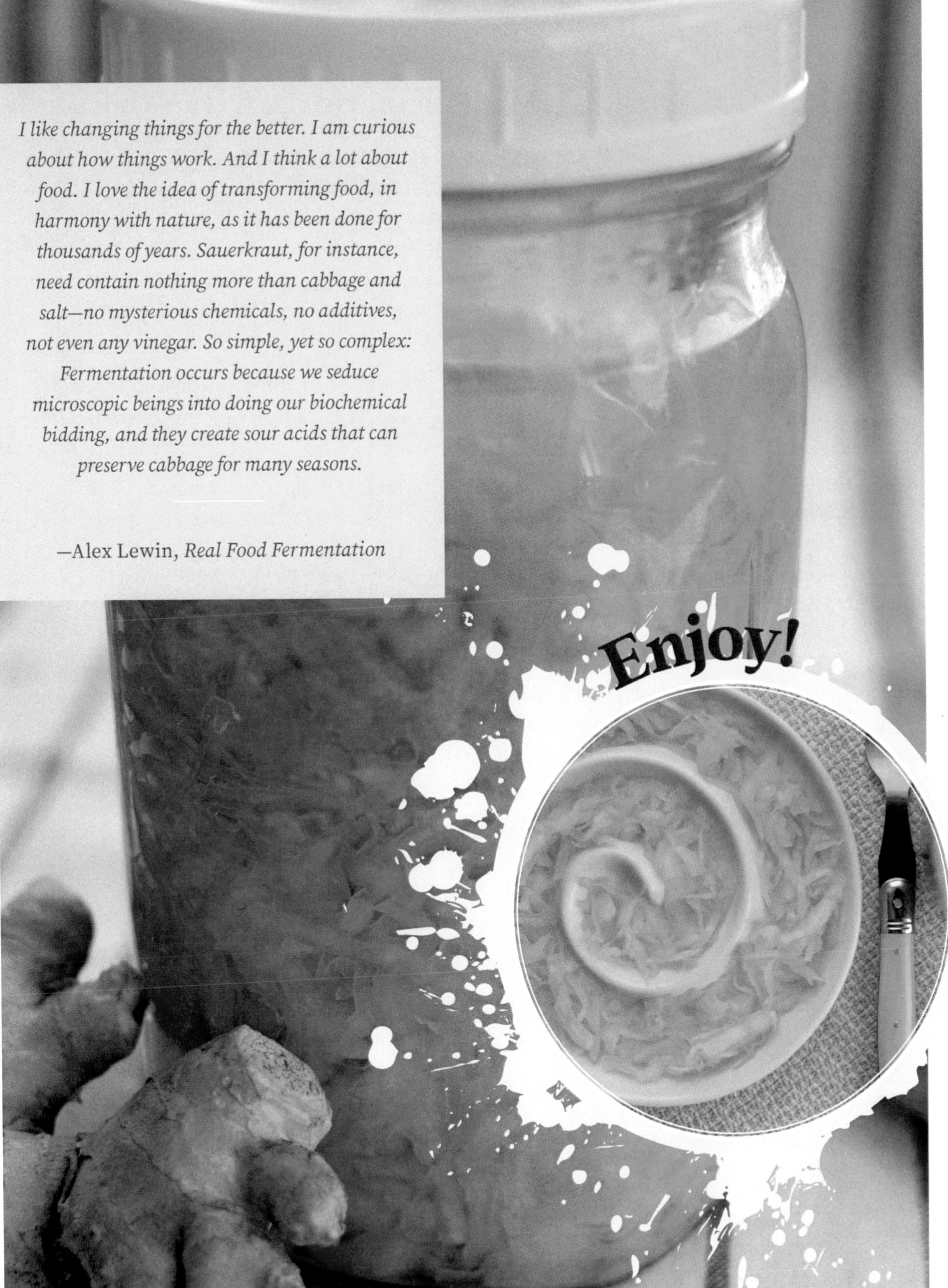

I like changing things for the better. I am curious about how things work. And I think a lot about food. I love the idea of transforming food, in harmony with nature, as it has been done for thousands of years. Sauerkraut, for instance, need contain nothing more than cabbage and salt—no mysterious chemicals, no additives, not even any vinegar. So simple, yet so complex: Fermentation occurs because we seduce microscopic beings into doing our biochemical bidding, and they create sour acids that can preserve cabbage for many seasons.

—Alex Lewin, *Real Food Fermentation*

Hawaiian Sauerkraut—With Turmeric for a Health Punch

Hawaiian Sauerkraut is a refreshing addition to any meal on a hot summer day. It also makes a great topping for a slice of Hawaiian or pepperoni pizza—don't knock it till you've tried it! Also try a ham roll-up: spread a thin slice of ham with cream cheese, add a bit of Hawaiian Sauerkraut (letting the brine drip off first), and roll up. Medicinally known for its anti-inflammatory, anticancer properties, turmeric is a great addition to sauerkraut. Research shows that curcumin, the active ingredient in turmeric, acts as a powerful antioxidant and also induces the flow of bile, to help break down fats.

A TIP FROM THE SAUERKRAUT

Turmeric root stains everything it comes in contact with. Wear thin disposable gloves, or mix the sauerkraut with a large spoon, which you can then use to pack it into the jar. To avoid staining your cutting board, place your box grater on a sheet of wax paper.

When I add fruit to a ferment, I shorten the fermentation time. The sugar from the pineapple gives the bacteria extra sugar to consume, and if left to ferment for too long, your ferment can shift toward the alcohol side.

MAKES 1 QUART (1 L) OF SAUERKRAUT TEEMING WITH TRILLIONS OF BENEFICIAL BACTERIA.

FERMENTATION TIME: 1–2 WEEKS

INGREDIENTS

1 cup (240 ml) fresh or frozen pineapple, roughly chopped

1 2-inch (5 cm) piece of fresh ginger root, peeled and finely grated

1 2-inch (5 cm) piece of fresh turmeric root, peeled and finely grated

¼ cup (60 ml) fresh cilantro, coarsely chopped

1 lime, zest and juice of

1 teaspoon (5 ml) turmeric powder

1 medium head fresh green cabbage, 2–3 pounds (1 kg)

1 tablespoon (15 ml) fine-grain iodine-free salt

INSTRUCTIONS

1 **SET UP.** Place your bowl on the scale. Either zero out the scale or write down the tare of your bowl.

2 **CHOP.** Prep your pineapple, ginger, turmeric, cilantro, and lime zest and add to your bowl along with the turmeric powder. Set aside a clean cabbage leaf for use in step 5. Quarter the cabbage, leaving the core in, and slice into thin strips until close to core, tossing the core. Add sliced cabbage to your bowl until the weight of the vegetables and cabbage is 1¾ pounds (28 oz or 800 g).

3 **SALT.** Sprinkle with 1 tablespoon salt—that's 16 grams (or 2%) by weight. Thoroughly mix until salt is well dispersed. Let sit at room temperature for 20 minutes to allow the salt to pull the water out of the vegetables. Then massage the cabbage with strong hands until it clumps together and a puddle of brine can be seen when tipping bowl to the side.

4 **PACK.** Pack mixture into your jar, pressing cabbage down tightly with your fist to allow the brine to rise. Leave 1½–2 inches (4–5 cm) of space between the top of your cabbage and the top of the jar.

5 **SUBMERGE AND SEAL.** Take the cabbage leaf saved in step 2, tear it to just fit inside the jar, and place it on top of the packed mixture. Using your preferred weight to hold the mixture below the brine, screw on lid or air lock lid of choice, following product directions. Label your jar with date and flavor.

6 **FERMENT.** Let ferment for 2–4 weeks. Place in a shallow bowl on your kitchen counter, out of direct sunlight—ideally between 65 and 72 °F (18–22 °C)—to ferment until texture and tang is to your liking.

7 **STORE.** Open the jar, remove the weight, and clean rim and jar. Firmly screw on storage lid. Add fermentation time to your label and place in your refrigerator.

> *Lacto-fermentation is basically a kind of carefully controlled decay. It is an adventure that is simultaneously magical, mysterious, and slightly dangerous. It is a kind of culinary frontier, and it is exciting to cross it. Because microorganisms aren't perceptible to the naked eye, they are rather alien beings, and most Americans growing up in a largely pasteurized, sterilized world are afraid of this unknown realm.*
>
> —Jessica Prentice, *Full Moon Feast: Food and the Hunger for Connection*

Enjoy!

Sweet Garlic Sauerkraut—Kid Friendly

This Sweet Garlic Sauerkraut recipe was inspired while doing a sauerkraut demonstration at a local farm. The only vegetables available were cabbage (of course), carrots, and garlic. I mixed them together into what has become my signature recipe.
The sweetness of the carrots contrasts nicely with the sharpness of the garlic in this recipe and is sure to please all palates. Many children find this to be their favorite sauerkraut.

MAKES 1 QUART (1 L) OF SAUERKRAUT TEEMING WITH TRILLIONS OF BENEFICIAL BACTERIA.

FERMENTATION TIME: 2–4 WEEKS

INGREDIENTS

2–3 carrots, peeled and grated

2–3 garlic cloves, finely minced

1 medium head fresh green cabbage, 2–3 pounds (1 kg)

1 tablespoon (15 ml) fine-grain iodine-free salt

INSTRUCTIONS

1 **SET UP.** Place your bowl on the scale. Either zero out the scale or write down the tare of your bowl.

2 **CHOP.** Prep your carrots and garlic and add to your bowl. Set aside a clean cabbage leaf for use in step 5. Quarter the cabbage, leaving the core in, and slice into thin strips until close to core, tossing the core. Add sliced cabbage to your bowl until the weight of the vegetables and cabbage is 1¾ pounds (28 oz or 800 g).

3 **SALT.** Sprinkle with 1 tablespoon salt—that's 16 grams (or 2%) by weight. Thoroughly mix until salt is well dispersed. Let sit at room temperature for 20 minutes to allow the salt to pull the water out of the vegetables. Then massage the cabbage with strong hands until it clumps together and a puddle of brine can be seen when tipping bowl to the side.

4 **PACK.** Pack mixture into your jar, pressing cabbage down tightly with your fist to allow the brine to rise. Leave 1½–2 inches (4–5 cm) of space between the top of your cabbage and the top of the jar.

5 **SUBMERGE AND SEAL.** Take the cabbage leaf saved in step 2, tear it to just fit inside the jar, and place it on top of the packed mixture. Using your preferred weight to hold the mixture below the brine, screw on lid or air lock lid of choice, following product directions. Label your jar with date and flavor.

6 **FERMENT.** Let ferment for 2–4 weeks. Place in a shallow bowl on your kitchen counter, out of direct sunlight—ideally between 65 and 72 °F (18–22 °C)—to ferment until texture and tang is to your liking.

7 **STORE.** Open the jar, remove the weight, and clean rim and jar. Firmly screw on storage lid. Add fermentation time to your label and place in your refrigerator.

Lacto-fermentation takes ordinary vegetables and makes them even more nutritious by adding vitamins, making the vitamins more bioavailable, and supercharging them with probiotics. Plus the veggies are bubbly, fizzy, and utterly delicious! Lacto-fermentation preserves them, so they can preserve you. I love that these special foods showed up to help me on my life's journey.

—Donna Schwenk, *Cultured Food for Life*

Enjoy!

Cinnamon Apple Sauerkraut—Sweet, Tangy, and Kid-Friendly

Use Cinnamon Apple Sauerkraut to make a quick and delicious kid-friendly salad. Toss together a few cups of sliced cabbage, a cup of sauerkraut, orange and apple chunks, and toasted pecans. Top with a quick olive-oil-and-honey dressing.

MAKES 1 QUART (1 L) OF SAUERKRAUT TEEMING WITH TRILLIONS OF BENEFICIAL BACTERIA.

FERMENTATION TIME: 1–2 WEEKS

INGREDIENTS

1 tart apple, peeled and finely diced

2–3 carrots, peeled and grated

1 2-inch (5 cm) piece of fresh ginger root, peeled and finely grated

1 teaspoon (5 ml) ground cinnamon

¼ cup (60 ml) raisins

1 medium head fresh green cabbage, 2–3 pounds (1 kg)

1 tablespoon (15 ml) fine-grain iodine-free salt

INSTRUCTIONS

1 **SET UP.** Place your bowl on the scale. Either zero out the scale or write down the tare of your bowl.

2 **CHOP.** Prep your apple, carrots, and ginger and add to your bowl along with the cinnamon and raisins. Set aside a clean cabbage leaf for use in step 5. Quarter the cabbage, leaving the core in, and slice into thin strips until close to core, tossing the core. Add sliced cabbage to your bowl until the weight of the vegetables and cabbage is 1¾ pounds (28 oz or 800 g).

3 **SALT.** Sprinkle with 1 tablespoon salt—that's 16 grams (or 2%) by weight. Thoroughly mix until salt is well dispersed. Let sit at room temperature for 20 minutes to allow the salt to pull the water out of the vegetables. Then massage the cabbage with strong hands until it clumps together and a puddle of brine can be seen when tipping bowl to the side.

4 **PACK.** Pack mixture into your jar, pressing cabbage down tightly with your fist to allow the brine to rise. Leave 1½–2 inches (4–5 cm) of space between the top of your cabbage and the top of the jar.

5 **SUBMERGE AND SEAL.** Take the cabbage leaf saved in step 2, tear it to just fit inside the jar, and place it on top of the packed mixture. Using your preferred weight to hold the mixture below the brine, screw on lid or air lock lid of choice, following product directions. Label your jar with date and flavor.

6 **FERMENT.** Let ferment for just 1–2 weeks due to the high sugar content of the apple which can speed up fermentation. Place in a shallow bowl on your kitchen counter, out of direct sunlight—ideally between 65 and 72 °F (18–22 °C)—to ferment until texture and tang is to your liking.

7 **STORE.** Open the jar, remove the weight, and clean rim and jar. Firmly screw on storage lid. Add fermentation time to your label and place in your refrigerator.

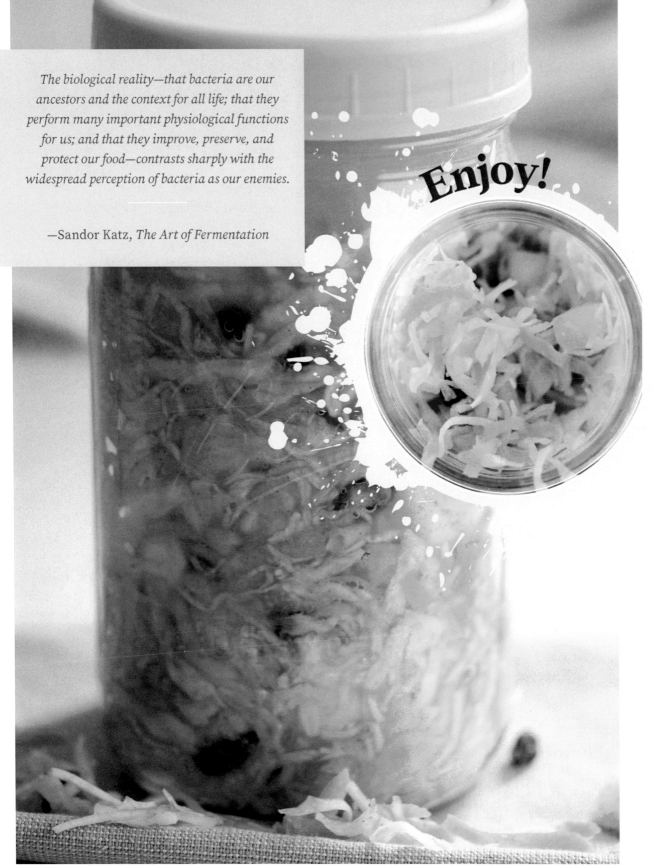

The biological reality—that bacteria are our ancestors and the context for all life; that they perform many important physiological functions for us; and that they improve, preserve, and protect our food—contrasts sharply with the widespread perception of bacteria as our enemies.

—Sandor Katz, *The Art of Fermentation*

Enjoy!

Sauerkraut Corn Relish—Summer Delight

When fresh peppers make their appearance at our local farmer's market, I usually make a few batches of Sauerkraut Corn Relish and use it for topping our summer hot dogs. The peppers will lose their color and soften over time, so I like to eat this sauerkraut within a few months.

A TIP FROM THE SAUERKRAUT WIZARD

With hot peppers, the heat is in the seeds and the inner membrane. Vary the heat by how many jalapeños you use, how many seeds you leave in, and whether you remove the inner membrane. Wash your hands well after handling hot peppers.

MAKES 1 QUART (1 L) OF SAUERKRAUT TEEMING WITH TRILLIONS OF BENEFICIAL BACTERIA.

FERMENTATION TIME: 1–2 WEEKS

INGREDIENTS

1 cup (240 ml) corn, sliced off fresh corn cobs or frozen

½ sweet red pepper, seeded and finely diced

1 jalapeño pepper, seeded and finely diced

1–2 stalks celery, finely diced

½ medium onion, finely diced

¼ cup (60 ml) fresh cilantro, coarsely chopped

½ teaspoon (2 ml) mustard seeds

1 small head fresh green cabbage, 1–1½ pounds (454–680 g)

1 tablespoon (15 ml) fine-grain iodine-free salt

INSTRUCTIONS

1 **SET UP.** Place your bowl on the scale. Either zero out the scale or write down the tare of your bowl.

2 **CHOP.** Prep your corn, red pepper, jalapeño pepper, celery, onion, and cilantro and add to your bowl along with the mustard seeds. Set aside a clean cabbage leaf for use in step 5. Quarter the cabbage, leaving the core in, and slice into thin strips until close to core, tossing the core. Add sliced cabbage to your bowl until the weight of the vegetables and cabbage is 1¾ pounds (28 oz or 800 g).

3 **SALT.** Sprinkle with 1 tablespoon salt—that's 16 grams (or 2%) by weight. Thoroughly mix until salt is well dispersed. Let sit at room temperature for 20 minutes to allow the salt to pull the water out of the vegetables. Then massage the cabbage with strong hands until it clumps together and a puddle of brine can be seen when tipping bowl to the side. *Note:* Due to the heat from the jalapeños, if you have sensitive hands, consider wearing gloves when mixing.

4 **PACK.** Pack mixture into your jar, pressing cabbage down tightly with your fist to allow the brine to rise. Leave 1½–2 inches (4–5 cm) of space between the top of your cabbage and the top of the jar.

5 **SUBMERGE AND SEAL.** Take the cabbage leaf saved in step 2, tear it to just fit inside the jar, and place it on top of the packed mixture. Using your preferred weight to hold the mixture below the brine, screw on lid or air lock lid of choice, following product directions. Label your jar with date and flavor.

6 **FERMENT.** Let ferment for just 1–2 weeks due to the high sugar content of the corn which can speed up fermentation. Place in a shallow bowl on your kitchen counter, out of direct sunlight—ideally between 65 and 72 °F (18–22 °C)—to ferment until texture and tang is to your liking.

7 **STORE.** Open the jar, remove the weight, and clean rim and jar. Firmly screw on storage lid. Add fermentation time to your label and place in your refrigerator.

> *And because fermentation is, by nature, an artisanal process, the disappearance of fermented foods has hastened the centralization and industrialization of our food supply, to the detriment of small farms and local economies.*
>
> —Sally Fallon Morell,
> quoted in *Wild Fermentation* by Sandor Katz

Enjoy!

Christmas Sauerkraut—Festive Holiday Flavors

Cranberry season generally begins in September and runs through December. If you see fresh cranberries at your farmer's market or in stores, grab a few bags. They freeze well and can be used for fermentation any time of the year.

Ferment Christmas Sauerkraut in early fall to enjoy with your holiday turkey.

MAKES 1 QUART (1 L) OF SAUERKRAUT TEEMING WITH TRILLIONS OF BENEFICIAL BACTERIA.

FERMENTATION TIME: 1–2 WEEKS

INGREDIENTS

1 cup (240 ml) fresh or frozen cranberries, roughly chopped

1 tart apple, peeled and finely diced

¼ cup (60 ml) dried cranberries

1 teaspoon (5 ml) ground cinnamon

3 whole star anise pods, or 1 teaspoon (5 ml) anise seed

1 medium head fresh green cabbage, 2–3 pounds (1 kg)

1 tablespoon (15 ml) fine-grain iodine-free salt

INSTRUCTIONS

1 **SET UP.** Place your bowl on the scale. Either zero out the scale or write down the tare of your bowl.

2 **CHOP.** Prep your fresh cranberries and apple and add to your bowl along with the dried cranberries, cinnamon, and anise. Set aside a clean cabbage leaf for use in step 5. Quarter the cabbage, leaving the core in, and slice into thin strips until close to core, tossing the core. Add sliced cabbage to your bowl until the weight of the vegetables and cabbage is 1¾ pounds (28 oz or 800 g).

3 **SALT.** Sprinkle with 1 tablespoon salt—that's 16 grams (or 2%) by weight. Thoroughly mix until salt is well dispersed. Let sit at room temperature for 20 minutes to allow the salt to pull the water out of the vegetables. Then massage the cabbage with strong hands until it clumps together and a puddle of brine can be seen when tipping bowl to the side.

4 **PACK.** Pack mixture into your jar, pressing cabbage down tightly with your fist to allow the brine to rise. Leave 1½–2 inches (4–5 cm) of space between the top of your cabbage and the top of the jar.

5 **SUBMERGE AND SEAL.** Take the cabbage leaf saved in step 2, tear it to just fit inside the jar, and place it on top of the packed mixture. Using your preferred weight to hold the mixture below the brine, screw on lid or air lock lid of choice, following product directions. Label your jar with date and flavor.

6 **FERMENT.** Let ferment for just 1–2 weeks due to the high sugar content of the apple which can speed up fermentation. Place in a shallow bowl on your kitchen counter, out of direct sunlight—ideally between 65 and 72 °F (18–22 °C)—to ferment until texture and tang is to your liking.

7 **STORE.** Open the jar, remove the weight, and clean rim and jar. Firmly screw on storage lid. Add fermentation time to your label and place in your refrigerator.

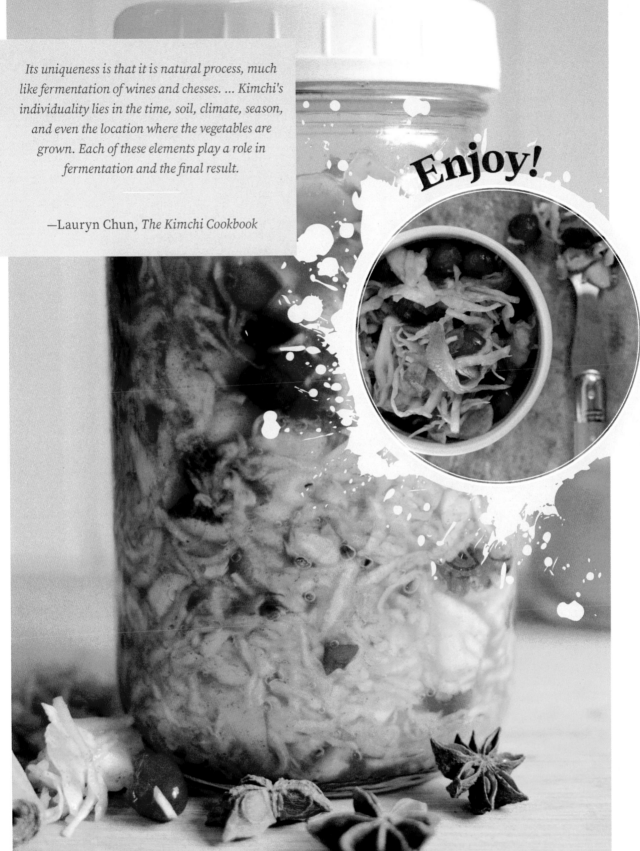

Its uniqueness is that it is natural process, much like fermentation of wines and chesses. ... Kimchi's individuality lies in the time, soil, climate, season, and even the location where the vegetables are grown. Each of these elements play a role in fermentation and the final result.

—Lauryn Chun, *The Kimchi Cookbook*

Enjoy!

CHAPTER 14

Sauerkraut Recipes with a Bit of Spicy Heat

BASEBALL SAUERKRAUT, (P.112)

FIRECRACKER SAUERKRAUT, (P.114)

KIMCHI-STYLE SAUERKRAUT, (P.116)

CURRY SAUERKRAUT, (P.118)

Baseball Sauerkraut—Home-Run Flavor Hit

Baseball season or not, one can always use a flavorful, relish-like sauerkraut recipe to add a special zing to a freshly grilled hot dog, barbecued hamburger, or just about anything.

When adding sauerkraut to a protein-rich meal, not only do you get the usual benefits—better digestion, increased nutrition, and support of your immune system—but the probiotics in sauerkraut greatly aid in the digestion of protein. A win-win situation.

Since this recipe is more like an onion relish than a sauerkraut, it breaks my general guidelines of keeping flavoring ingredients to 25% of the total weight, with sliced cabbage making up the remainder. Rest assured, even though you use close to a pound of onions, it ferments just fine.

MAKES 1 QUART (1 L) OF SAUERKRAUT TEEMING WITH TRILLIONS OF BENEFICIAL BACTERIA.

FERMENTATION TIME: 1–2 WEEKS

INGREDIENTS

2 white onions (baseball size), finely diced

1 sweet red pepper, seeded and finely diced

1 jalapeño pepper, seeded and finely diced

1 tablespoon (15 ml) paprika

½ teaspoon (2 ml) mustard seeds

½ teaspoon (2 ml) celery seeds

1 small head fresh green cabbage, 1–1½ pounds (454–680 g)

1 tablespoon (15 ml) fine-grain iodine-free salt

INSTRUCTIONS

1 **SET UP.** Place your bowl on the scale. Either zero out the scale or write down the tare of your bowl.

2 **CHOP.** Prep your white onions, red pepper, and jalapeño pepper and add to your bowl along with the mustard seeds and celery seeds. Set aside a clean cabbage leaf for use in step 5. Quarter the cabbage, leaving the core in, and slice into thin strips until close to core, tossing the core. Add sliced cabbage to your bowl until the weight of the vegetables and cabbage is 1¾ pounds (28 oz or 800 g).

3 **SALT.** Sprinkle with 1 tablespoon salt—that's 16 grams (or 2%) by weight. Thoroughly mix until salt is well dispersed. Let sit at room temperature for 20 minutes to allow the salt to pull the water out of the vegetables. Then massage the cabbage with strong hands until it clumps together and a puddle of brine can be seen when tipping bowl to the side. *Note:* Due to the heat from the jalapeños, if you have sensitive hands, consider wearing gloves when mixing.

4 **PACK.** Pack mixture into your jar, pressing cabbage down tightly with your fist to allow the brine to rise. Leave 1½–2 inches (4–5 cm) of space between the top of your cabbage and the top of the jar.

5 **SUBMERGE AND SEAL.** Take the cabbage leaf saved in step 2, tear it to just fit inside the jar, and place it on top of the packed mixture. Using your preferred weight to hold the mixture below the brine, screw on lid or air lock lid of choice, following product directions. Label your jar with date and flavor.

6 **FERMENT.** Let ferment for 2–4 weeks. Place in a shallow bowl on your kitchen counter, out of direct sunlight—ideally between 65 and 72 °F (18–22 °C)—to ferment until texture and tang is to your liking.

7 **STORE.** Open the jar, remove the weight, and clean rim and jar. Firmly screw on storage lid. Add fermentation time to your label and place in your refrigerator.

The word ferment comes from the Latin root fervere, which means "to boil." You will see soon enough that this is an apt description for fermentation! Fermenting foods can indeed appear to be boiling. Not only does the action of fermentation heat up the food, but an effervescence builds up from the gases given off by fermenting organisms. I myself have created some incredible happy, bubbly sauerkraut.

—Wardeh Harmon,
The Complete Idiot's Guide to Fermenting Foods

Enjoy!

Firecracker Sauerkraut—Turn Up the Heat to Your Liking

Firecracker Sauerkraut goes well with Mexican, South American, and Thai cuisine, or with any dish that you would add jalapeños to.

A TIP FROM THE SAUERKRAUT WIZARD

With hot peppers, the heat is in the seeds and the inner membrane. Vary the heat by how many jalapeños you use, how many seeds you leave in, and whether you remove the inner membrane. Wash your hands well after handling hot peppers.

MAKES 1 QUART (1 L) OF SAUERKRAUT TEEMING WITH TRILLIONS OF BENEFICIAL BACTERIA.

FERMENTATION TIME: 2–4 WEEKS

INGREDIENTS

¼ medium red onion, thinly sliced

1–3 jalapeño peppers, seeded and sliced

1 teaspoon (5 ml) dried oregano

1 teaspoon (5 ml) cumin seeds

¼ teaspoon (1 ml) dried red pepper flakes

1 medium head fresh green cabbage, 2–3 pounds (1 kg)

1 tablespoon (15 ml) fine-grain iodine-free salt

INSTRUCTIONS

1 **SET UP.** Place your bowl on the scale. Either zero out the scale or write down the tare of your bowl.

2 **CHOP.** Prep your red onion and jalapeño pepper(s) and add to your bowl along with the dried oregano, cumin seeds, and red pepper flakes. Set aside a clean cabbage leaf for use in step 5. Quarter the cabbage, leaving the core in, and slice into thin ribbons until close to core, discarding the core. Add sliced cabbage to your bowl until the weight of the vegetables and cabbage is 1¾ pounds (28 oz or 800 g).

3 **SALT.** Sprinkle with 1 tablespoon salt—that's 16 grams (or 2%) by weight. Thoroughly mix until salt is well dispersed. Let sit at room temperature for 20 minutes to allow the salt to pull the water out of the vegetables. Then massage the cabbage with strong hands until it clumps together and a puddle of brine can be seen when tipping bowl to the side. *Note:* Due to the heat from the jalapeños, if you have sensitive hands, consider wearing gloves when mixing.

4 **PACK.** Pack mixture into your jar, pressing cabbage down tightly with your fist to allow the brine to rise. Leave 1½–2 inches (4–5 cm) of space between the top of your cabbage and the top of the jar.

5 **SUBMERGE AND SEAL.** Take the cabbage leaf saved in step 2, tear it to just fit inside the jar, and place it on top of the packed mixture. Using your preferred weight to hold the mixture below the brine, screw on lid or air lock lid of choice, following product directions. Label your jar with date and flavor.

6 **FERMENT.** Let ferment for 2–4 weeks. Place in a shallow bowl on your kitchen counter, out of direct sunlight—ideally between 65 and 72 °F (18–22 °C)—to ferment until texture and tang is to your liking.

7 **STORE.** Open the jar, remove the weight, and clean rim and jar. Firmly screw on storage lid. Add fermentation time to your label and place in your refrigerator

To ferment food is to predigest it, in effect, breaking long chains of proteins, fats, and carbohydrates our bodies might not be able to make good use of into simpler, safer compounds that they can. Think of the kraut crock as a bubbling auxiliary stomach, doing much of the work of digestion before your body has to.

—Michael Pollan, *Cooked*

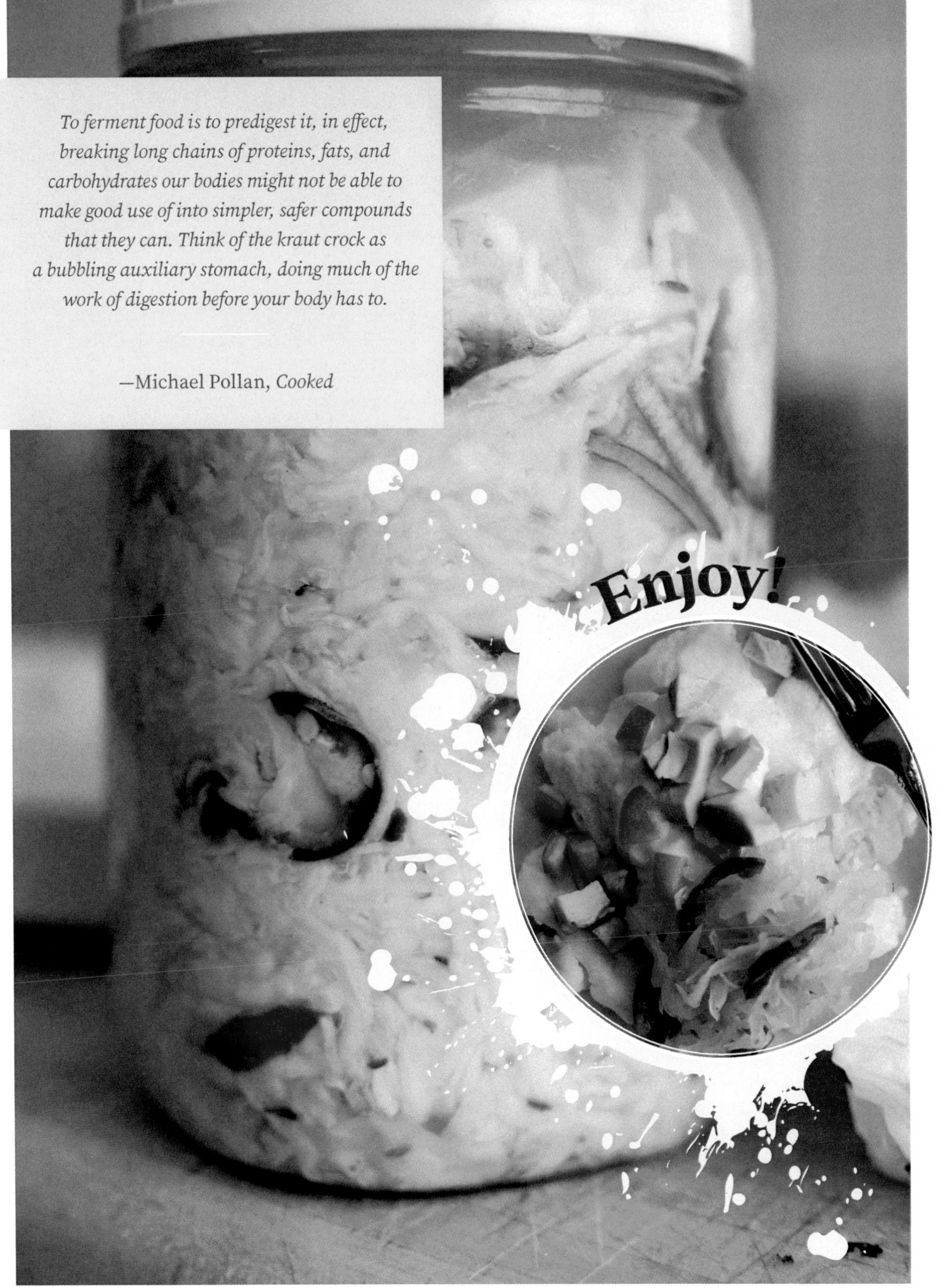

Kimchi-Style Sauerkraut—A Spicy Depth of Flavor

Traditionally, kimchi is made with napa cabbage that is first soaked in a salty brine. The rinsed cabbage is then mixed with a garlic-ginger-red pepper paste, along with a fermented fish sauce, and then packed into an earthenware crock. For this sauerkraut recipe, we instead use green cabbage, mixing in the traditional ingredients (omitting the fermented fish sauce) and salt to create our brine in the bowl in one step.

A TIP FROM THE SAUERKRAUT WIZARD
It is worth going out of your way to purchase *gochugaru*, or Korean red pepper powder. Gochugaru is a coarsely ground red pepper with a texture between flakes and powder. It disperses throughout your sauerkraut, coloring it beautifully and adding a complex flavor not found with red pepper flakes. The highest quality gochugaru is made from sun-dried chili peppers. For recommended brands, visit my Shop page at this shortened URL: **fmeasy.me/kimchi**

MAKES 1 QUART (1 L) OF SAUERKRAUT TEEMING WITH TRILLIONS OF BENEFICIAL BACTERIA.
FERMENTATION TIME: 2–4 WEEKS

INGREDIENTS

1–2 carrots, peeled and grated

1 large radish, peeled and grated—approx. ½ cup (120 ml)

1 bunch green onions, thinly sliced

1 2-inch (5 cm) piece fresh ginger root, peeled and finely grated

2–3 garlic cloves, finely minced

1 tablespoon (15 ml) gochugaru (Korean red pepper powder), or substitute ½–1 teaspoon (2–5 ml) red pepper flakes

1 medium head fresh green cabbage, 2–3 pounds (1 kg)

1 tablespoon (15 ml) fine-grain iodine-free salt

INSTRUCTIONS

1 **SET UP.** Place your bowl on the scale. Either zero out the scale or write down the tare of your bowl.

2 **CHOP.** Prep your carrots, radish, green onions, ginger, and garlic and add to your bowl along with the red pepper. Set aside a clean cabbage leaf for use in step 5. Quarter the cabbage, leaving the core in, and slice into thin strips until close to core, tossing the core. Add sliced cabbage to your bowl until the weight of the vegetables and cabbage is 1¾ pounds (28 oz or 800 g).

3 **SALT.** Sprinkle with 1 tablespoon salt—that's 16 grams (or 2%) by weight. Thoroughly mix until salt is well dispersed. Let sit at room temperature for 20 minutes to allow the salt to pull the water out of the vegetables. Then massage the cabbage with strong hands until it clumps together and a puddle of brine can be seen when tipping bowl to the side. *Note:* Due to the heat from the red pepper, if you have sensitive hands, consider wearing gloves when mixing.

4 **PACK.** Pack mixture into your jar, pressing cabbage down tightly with your fist to allow the brine to rise. Leave 1½–2 inches (4–5 cm) of space between the top of your cabbage and the top of the jar.

5 **SUBMERGE AND SEAL.** Take the cabbage leaf saved in step 2, tear it to just fit inside the jar, and place it on top of the packed mixture. Using your preferred weight to hold the mixture below the brine, screw on lid or air lock lid of choice, following product directions. Label your jar with date and flavor.

6 **FERMENT.** Let ferment for 2–4 weeks. Place in a shallow bowl on your kitchen counter, out of direct sunlight—ideally between 65 and 72 °F (18–22 °C)—to ferment until texture and tang is to your liking.

7 **STORE.** Open the jar, remove the weight, and clean rim and jar. Firmly screw on storage lid. Add fermentation time to your label and place in your refrigerator.

> *Learn how to cook—try new recipes, learn from your mistakes, be fearless, and above all, have fun!*
>
> —Julia Child

Enjoy!

Curry Sauerkraut—Teeming with Golden Brightness

Curry is a mixture of spices that contains turmeric, which contributes a bright yellow color to the powder. Turmeric contains curcumin, a substance with powerful anti-inflammatory and antioxidant properties, which is made more bioavailable by fermentation. The black pepper in curry powder enhances absorption. Curry Sauerkraut pairs nicely with Indian and Thai cuisine.

MAKES 1 QUART (1 L) OF SAUERKRAUT TEEMING WITH TRILLIONS OF BENEFICIAL BACTERIA.
FERMENTATION TIME: 2–4 WEEKS

INGREDIENTS

1–2 stalks celery, thinly sliced
2–3 carrots, peeled and grated
½ bunch green onions, thinly sliced
¼ medium onion, finely diced
1 tablespoon (15 ml) curry powder
1 medium head fresh green cabbage, 2–3 pounds (1 kg)
1 tablespoon (15 ml) fine-grain iodine-free salt

INSTRUCTIONS

1. **SET UP.** Place your bowl on the scale. Either zero out the scale or write down the tare of your bowl.
2. **CHOP.** Prep your celery, carrots, green onions, and onion and add to your bowl along with the curry powder. Set aside a clean cabbage leaf for use in step 5. Quarter the cabbage, leaving the core in, and slice into thin strips until close to core, tossing the core. Add sliced cabbage to your bowl until the weight of the vegetables and cabbage is 1¾ pounds (28 oz or 800 g).
3. **SALT.** Sprinkle with 1 tablespoon salt—that's 16 grams (or 2%) by weight. Thoroughly mix until salt is well dispersed. Let sit at room temperature for 20 minutes to allow the salt to pull the water out of the vegetables. Then massage the cabbage with strong hands until it clumps together and a puddle of brine can be seen when tipping bowl to the side. *Note:* Due to the heat from the curry powder, if you have sensitive hands, consider wearing gloves when mixing.
4. **PACK.** Pack mixture into your jar, pressing cabbage down tightly with your fist to allow the brine to rise. Leave 1½–2 inches (4–5 cm) of space between the top of your cabbage and the top of the jar.
5. **SUBMERGE AND SEAL.** Take the cabbage leaf saved in step 2, tear it to just fit inside the jar, and place it on top of the packed mixture. Using your preferred weight to hold the mixture below the brine, screw on lid or air lock lid of choice, following product directions. Label your jar with date and flavor.
6. **FERMENT.** Let ferment for 2–4 weeks. Place in a shallow bowl on your kitchen counter, out of direct sunlight—ideally between 65 and 72 °F (18–22 °C)—to ferment until texture and tang is to your liking.
7. **STORE.** Open the jar, remove the weight, and clean rim and jar. Firmly screw on storage lid. Add fermentation time to your label and place in your refrigerator.

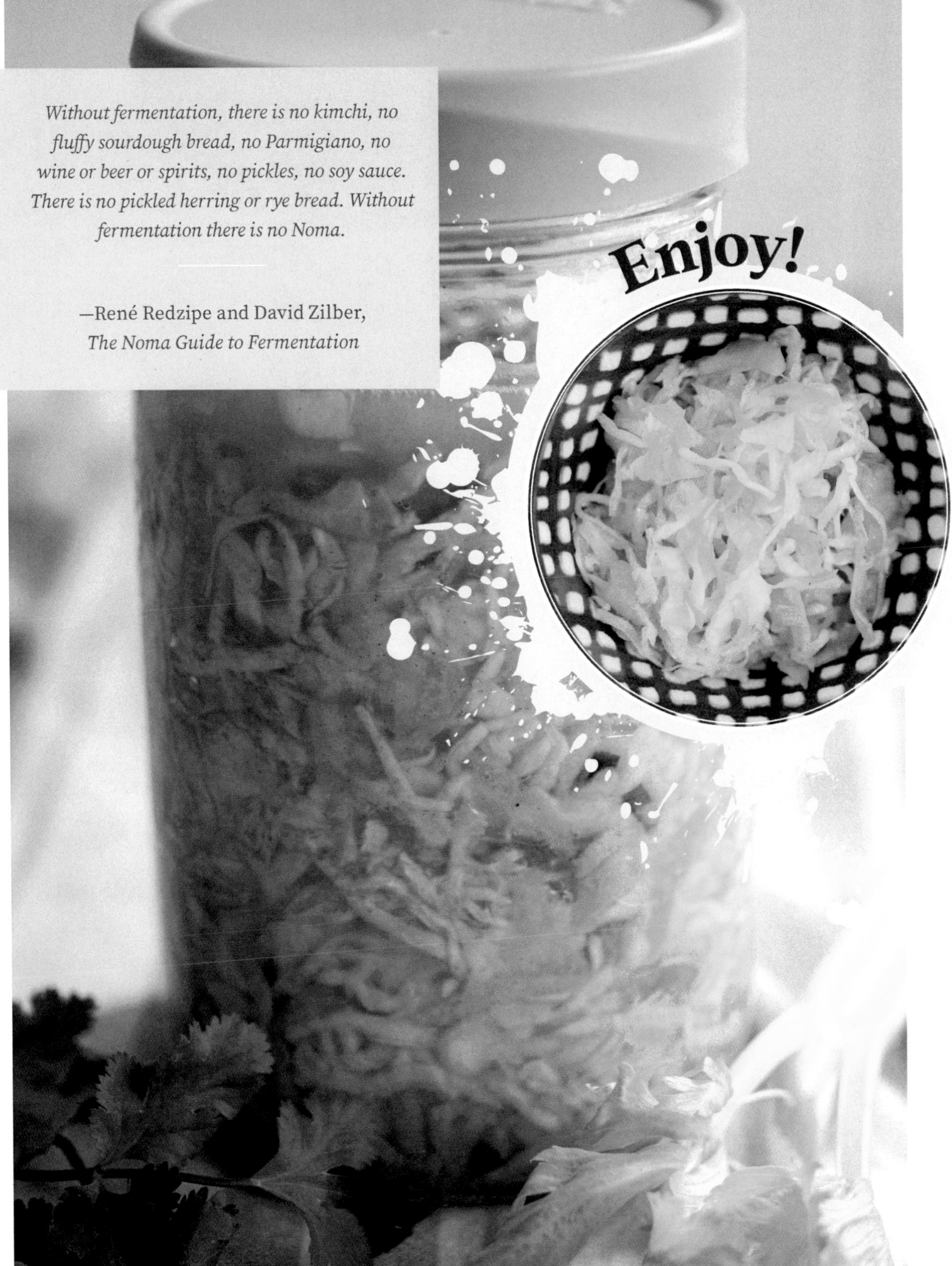

Without fermentation, there is no kimchi, no fluffy sourdough bread, no Parmigiano, no wine or beer or spirits, no pickles, no soy sauce. There is no pickled herring or rye bread. Without fermentation there is no Noma.

—René Redzipe and David Zilber,
The Noma Guide to Fermentation

PART 5

Not Just a Topping for Hot Dogs

You know that sauerkraut is rich in probiotics and valuable enzymes and is great for gut health, yet you may be hesitant to start incorporating this new food into your diet. After all, I'm asking you to eat a food that you've left on your counter for weeks. Relax. With a jar of sauerkraut at the ready in your refrigerator, you will be able to effortlessly add an extra dimension to any meal, unlocking flavors you never knew existed and reaping the added bonus of improved digestion to supercharge your health. No complex recipes are required.

CHAPTER 15

Effortlessly Adding Sauerkraut to Any Meal

Congratulations!

YOU HAVE FERMENTED A BATCH—OR MANY BATCHES—OF SAUERKRAUT. IT IS NOW TIME TO ENJOY THE FRUITS OF YOUR LABOR. A FEW GUIDELINES:

- **Keep it simple.** You can come up with all sorts of creative recipes for eating sauerkraut, but the simplest is alongside any meal or mixed into a salad. Feel no pressure to move beyond such simplicity.
- **Start consumption slowly.** If this is the first time for you to eat sauerkraut, go slow, especially if you have compromised digestion. If you experience gas, diarrhea, or other digestive symptoms, you've most likely introduced more bacteria and fiber into your diet than your body could handle. Scale back on your consumption. See Appendix 1: Daily Dosage (p.129) for further guidelines.
- **Serve straight from the jar.** Place a couple of jars of sauerkraut on the table and let each member of your family use their clean fork to put some of their favorite sauerkraut on their plate.
- **Let sauerkraut come to room temperature.** Most don't like to eat cold sauerkraut, so either remove it from the refrigerator an hour before the meal, or at the beginning of your meal place a serving on your plate and give it a bit of time to come to room temperature. Placing it on top of a warm dish is another way to take the chill out. Flavors will be more pronounced once sauerkraut has reached room temperature.

- **Rinse off excess salt.** If your sauerkraut is too salty, you can give it a quick rinse just before eating. This will wash off some but not all of the beneficial bacteria.
- **Use your leftover brine.** If you're lucky enough to still have brine when you get to the bottom of a jar, drink its probiotic-rich goodness, use it in place of vinegar in a salad dressing, or pour it into another finished ferment in your fridge.
- **Retain beneficial probiotics and enzymes.** If you want to take advantage the benefits of lacto-fermented sauerkraut, don't heat your sauerkraut over 105 °F (41 °C). Stirring sauerkraut into a warm bowl of soup or sprinkling some on top of your meal will slightly warm the sauerkraut but not damage the probiotics.
- **Cook with sauerkraut.** There are many traditional cooked dishes in which sauerkraut is an essential ingredient. Though enzymes and probiotics will be destroyed by the cooking process, fiber, nutrients, and flavors will be retained. To aid digestion, serve some raw sauerkraut alongside.

SAUERKRAUT FUN FACT

Americans consume 387 million pounds of sauerkraut annually, or 1.5 pounds per person per year. In Germany, the average per capita consumption of sauerkraut is approximately 2.6 pounds, down from 4.4 pounds 40 years ago. In Korea, they consume a whopping 49 pounds of kimchi per person per year.

Here are five simple ways to enjoy your tasty, probiotic-rich sauerkraut.

ENHANCE THE FLAVOR OF ANY MEAL

The easiest way to add sauerkraut to your diet is to serve it alongside any meal. Just place a few forkfuls of sauerkraut on your plate and enjoy with your meal. It is when you have a selection of sauerkraut flavors to choose from that putting together a meal becomes a fun and flavorful adventure. Here are a few of my favorite combinations:

- Roast turkey or chicken with Thyme for Leeks Sauerkraut
- Scrambled eggs with Kimchi-Style Sauerkraut
- Tacos with Firecracker Sauerkraut
- Pizza with Hawaiian Sauerkraut

MAKE AN ALMOST INSTANT SALAD

Sauerkraut adds a nice zing to any salad. Go simple and just throw together what you have on hand, or make a meal out of it.

What's in My Fridge Salad Bowl. In a bowl, mix lettuce, a few forkfuls of sauerkraut, some brine, a splash of olive oil, a squeeze of lemon, and freshly ground black pepper. For a more filling salad, add chunks of cheese or leftover meat. Nuts or dried cranberries are also a nice addition.

USE AS A CLASSIC OR NOT-SO-CLASSIC TOPPING

A hot dog, a hamburger, eggs, or even pizza all taste so much better with a topping of sauerkraut. Some of my favorites to have on hand for adding instant pizzazz to these foods are Firecracker Sauerkraut, Baseball Park Sauerkraut, and Hawaiian Sauerkraut.

SAUERKRAUT FUN FACT

In order for the German immigrants who landed in New York City in the 1860s to make a living, they began selling their sauerkraut with sausages and milk rolls from pushcarts in the Bowery, the southern portion of New York City. Eventually, the bun-and-sausage combination became a treat commonly known as hot dogs. To this day, a New York–style hot dog is served with sauerkraut.

ADD TO A SANDWICH, WRAP, LUNCH BOWL, OR BURRITO

Sauerkraut adds a pleasant zing to any sandwich, wrap, taco, or burrito. No matter what you put in there—veggies, cheeses, meats, relishes—a few forkfuls of sauerkraut will bring flavors to a new level. To avoid creating a soggy mess, use a fork to remove sauerkraut from the jar, letting excess brine drip off.

EAT IT STRAIGHT FROM THE JAR

Have that afternoon slump and wish you could take a nap? Hungry for something but don't know what? Try a few bites of sauerkraut—yes, you can eat it right out of the jar—and see if you are not soon re-energized and cravings go away.

SAUERKRAUT FUN FACT

Eating pork and sauerkraut on New Year's Day is a long-standing tradition both in Germany and Pennsylvania, to ensure as much goodness and wealth in the new year as the number of shreds of cabbage in the pot of sauerkraut. This was a German custom brought over by the Pennsylvania Dutch, who settled largely in the central portions of Pennsylvania.

AFTERWORD

5 Things I Wish I Had Known Before Embarking on My Fermentation Journey

Little did I know over fifteen years ago when I fermented my first batch of sauerkraut, following a recipe in the book *Nourishing Traditions* by Sally Fallon, that today I would find myself helping thousands of people from around the world learn how to ferment. A few of my treasured discoveries:

1. OUR VEGETABLES COME WITH EVERYTHING THEY NEED FOR FERMENTATION TO HAPPEN

Pause and ponder this for a moment: there are bacteria literally everywhere. But instead of embracing and trusting in the wonder of these microscopic creatures, we dive-bomb them with hand sanitizers and toxic cleaning products. We kill off both the good and the bad when we take a round of antibiotics for the slightest sniffle. And we live in fear of these microscopic beings.

Welcoming the world of fermentation into your home is your first small step toward accepting these little creatures into your life. Gradually, you will come to realize just how important they are, and that you are not the one making fermentation happen—the bacteria are.

So, no need to buy a nice little package of starter bacteria. No need to drip a tub of yogurt to obtain whey. Just cabbage, salt, and time is enough to not only ferment something fabulous but to develop a deep sense of awe of our microscopic friends.

2. FERMENTATION BEST UNFOLDS AT A SET SALINITY AND TEMPERATURE RANGE

Moldy, mushy batches of sauerkraut early on in my fermentation journey had me searching for solutions. With some research, I learned just how picky the bacteria responsible for fermentation are about their working conditions. They work best with just the right amount of salt and in a room that is neither too warm nor too cold. By weighing my ingredients—and salt—and not fermenting during the heat of summer, I keep the bacteria happy, as well as my taste buds!

3. TO CATCH THE BACTERIA AT THEIR BEST, FERMENT SEASONALLY WITH LOCAL PRODUCE

Dull, yellowed, old cabbage or vegetables past their prime are not only lacking in nutrients but have started rotting, and will most likely not ferment into a finished product with the greatest range of probiotics and complex flavors. By allowing what you find fresh in the store, at the farmer's market, or harvested from your garden dictate what you'll be fermenting, not only does the fermentation process unfold beautifully, but you soon anticipate the arrival of the first spring vegetables with the same excitement with whichyou anticipated an upcoming holiday as a child.

4. A FEW FERMENTATION TOOLS DO MAKE FERMENTATION MORE PLEASURABLE

With the rise in popularity of fermentation, it's easy to get carried away buying the latest shiny object. If I had to limit myself to just three tools, I would buy the My Weigh KD-8000 Digital Scale (to ensure I use the correct amount of salt), the 3-Pack Pickle Helix Fermentation Kit by Trellis & Co. (to keep my small batches of ferments anaerobic), and a water-sealed fermentation crock (to seasonally ferment large batches of sauerkraut).

5. THERE IS GREAT JOY IN EFFORTLESSLY ADDING THE WOW! FACTOR TO YOUR MEALS

It starts with a dollop of simple sauerkraut on your plate. Wow! Soon you branch out and try new flavors of sauerkraut, and before you know it your taste buds are begging for more.

You then move beyond sauerkraut and perhaps ferment some cucumber pickles, carrot sticks, or julienned beets. Suddenly, salads topped with these flavors go pop. And sandwiches are taken to a new level with your small arsenal of flavoring pastes.

Now there is a whole shelf in your refrigerator devoted to your ferments: Fermented Garlic Paste to stir into sautéed greens or spread on a piece of buttered toast. Pepper Relish to flavor deviled eggs or egg salad sandwiches. Cranberry Relish for serving alongside turkey or stirring into yogurt. Leek Paste to add a depth of flavor to soups or spread on a ham sandwich.

Enjoy the journey. Soon, you too will have a stash of "fast-food jars" in your fridge, and before you know it, you'll be effortlessly enjoying something fermented with just about every meal.

APPENDIXES

Appendix 1

DAILY DOSAGE: HOW MUCH SAUERKRAUT SHOULD I EAT?

Sauerkraut is packed with high concentrations of beneficial bacteria. This is good, and most can handle the influx of probiotics. But for some, *excessive* consumption of sauerkraut can destabilize their gut microbiome—exactly the opposite of what many of us are trying to achieve by eating sauerkraut. So, when it comes to deciding how much sauerkraut to eat, think condiment. Sauerkraut is best eaten in small portions. Put a few forkfuls of sauerkraut on your plate with any meal. Add a bit when putting together a salad or when making a sandwich, hamburger, or hot dog.

Start slow and pay attention to any digestive symptoms, especially if this is the first time for you to eat sauerkraut. If there are rumblings in your tummy, you know you've eaten more than your digestive system is ready for. Give your gut time to get used to this new food.

SAUERKRAUT FUN FACT

Excessive consumption of sauerkraut may lead to bloating and flatulence due to too much raffinose, a trisaccharide—composed of galactose, glucose, and fructose—that the human small intestine cannot break down.

Here are some basic guidelines to follow.

DIGESTIVE ISSUES? NEVER EATEN FERMENTED FOODS?

If you have compromised digestion or difficulty digesting fiber, start first with just a sip or two of the brine and then move up to eating a small bite of the sauerkraut, watching for symptoms. Take about a month to work your way up to two forkfuls of sauerkraut per day.

GOOD HEALTH BUT NEVER EATEN FERMENTED FOODS?

Start with one forkful once a day and work your way up to one to two forkfuls twice a day. This will give your body time to get used to the influx of valuable probiotics.

ALREADY EAT A VARIETY OF FERMENTED FOODS?

Start with one to two forkfuls once a day, gradually working your way up to two to three forkfuls with two to three meals a day.

Appendix 2

SALT CHART: HOW MUCH SALT DO I ADD?

There are three ways to measure how much salt to add to your bowl of sliced cabbage: by weight, volume, or taste.

MEASURE SALT BY WEIGHT—MOST ACCURATE

Use a gram scale to weigh a precise percentage of salt for the amount of sliced cabbage and flavoring ingredients in your ferment. Since a tablespoon of coarse salt will weigh more than a tablespoon of fine-grain salt, this method works with all densities and grains of salt.

For a safe fermentation, stay within a 1.5–2.5% range. Start with 2.0% salinity and adjust slightly for future batches if necessary.

GRAMS OF SALT TO USE FOR WEIGHT OF INGREDIENTS

PERCENT SALINITY DESIRED	1¾ POUNDS	800 GRAMS	5 POUNDS (TRIPLE BATCH)	2.4 KILOGRAMS (TRIPLE BATCH)
1.50%	12 grams	12 grams	34 grams	36 grams
1.75%	14 grams	14 grams	40 grams	42 grams
2.00%	16 grams	16 grams	45 grams	48 grams
2.25%	18 grams	18 grams	51 grams	54 grams
2.50%	20 grams	20 grams	57 grams	60 grams

A triple batch is useful when filling a crock. Mix and make successive 5-pound (2.4 kg) batches until your crock is 75–80% full.

To calculate how much salt to use on your own, multiply the weight of ingredients in grams by the percent salinity desired. For example, to calculate 1.5% salinity, first convert the percentage to a decimal (0.015). Then multiply the weight of your batch in grams (1200, for example) by your decimal: 1200 × 0.015 = 18 grams of salt.

MEASURE SALT BY VOLUME—FAIRLY ACCURATE

Use a measuring spoon to measure a set volume of salt for the amount of cabbage you have sliced. Be aware that you can easily end up with a 30% difference in how much salt you add, due to variances in the grain size between a coarse-grain salt and a fine-grain salt, the moisture content of your salt, how full you fill your measuring spoon, and the accuracy of your measuring spoon. In addition, there are differently sized measuring spoons around the world. In Australia a tablespoon measures 20 milliliters; in Great Britain, 17.7 milliliters; and in North America and elsewhere, 14.7 milliliters.

For a 1-quart (1 L) batch, prepare 1¾ pounds (28 oz or 800 g) of sliced cabbage and flavoring ingredients. Add 1 tablespoon (14.7 ml) of salt.

To fill a crock, prepare 5 pounds (2.4 kg) of sliced cabbage and flavoring ingredients. Add 3 tablespoons (44 ml) of salt.

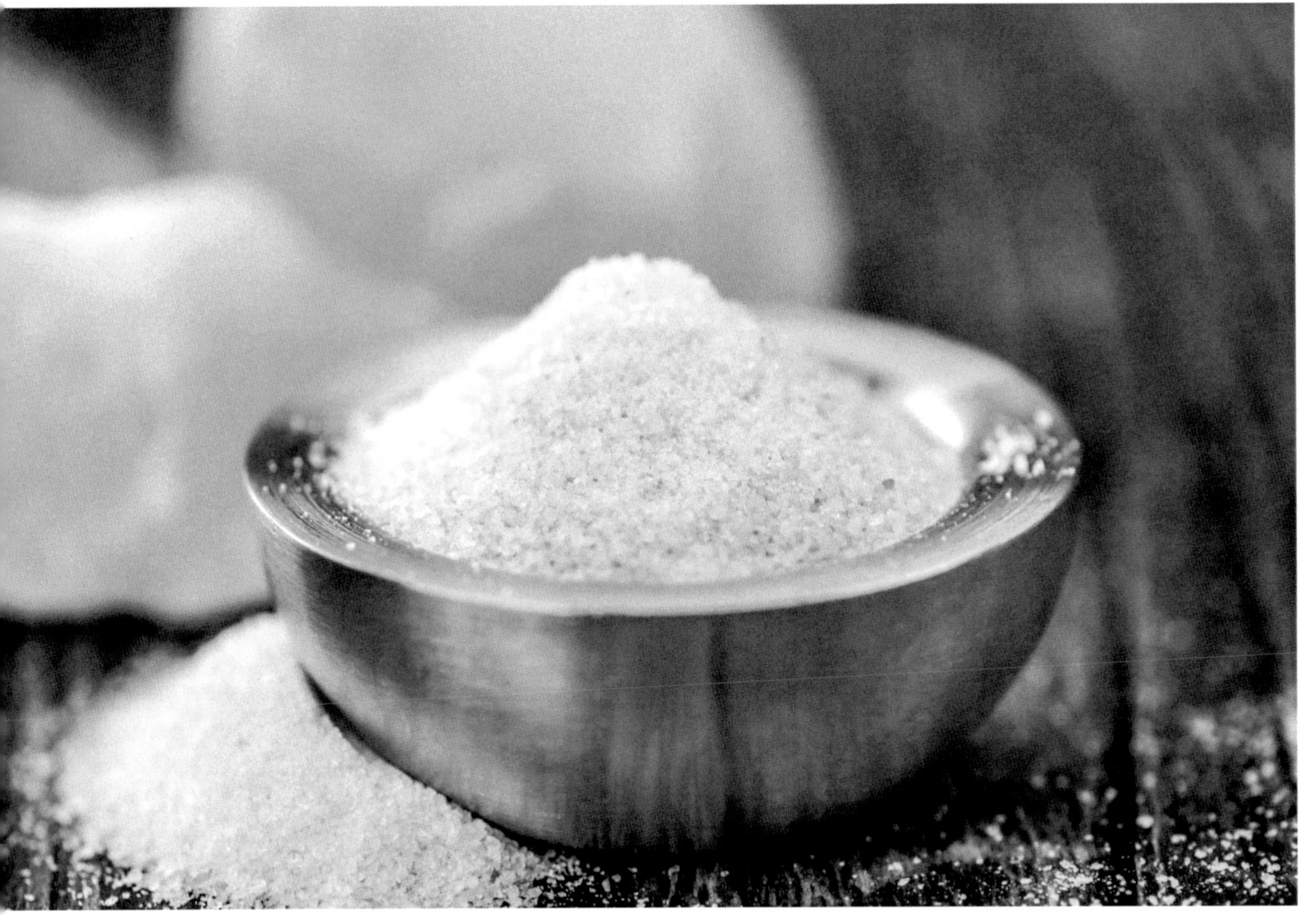

MEASURE SALT BY TASTE—LEAST ACCURATE

Use your taste buds to determine if you have added the right amount of salt to your cabbage and vegetable mixture. Since taste buds vary from person to person and from day to day, there can be a great variance in how much salt is added, and it can be difficult to get consistent batches.

For a 1-quart (1 L) batch, prepare 1–2 pounds (454–907 g) of sliced cabbage and flavoring ingredients. Add just under 1 tablespoon (14 g) of salt, mix well, then taste. You want it to taste as salty as a potato chip, but not as salty as seawater. If necessary, adjust by adding more sliced cabbage or more salt, then mix well and taste again.

Glossary

Aerobic. A fermentation environment *with* air. The fermentations of kombucha, sourdough bread, and milk kefir are examples of aerobic fermentation processes.

Anaerobic. A fermentation environment *without* air. The fermentations of sauerkraut, pickles, and kimchi are examples of anaerobic fermentation processes.

Bioavailability. The degree to which food nutrients are absorbed and utilized in the body. Fermentation makes nutrients more bioavailable.

Botulism. A potentially deadly illness caused by a toxin produced by the bacteria *Clostridium botulinum.* It is impossible for the bacterium responsible for botulism to make its very dangerous spores in the low pH of lacto-fermented vegetables.

Brine. A salty solution for pickling or fermenting.

Culture. See **Starter culture.**

Gochugaru. Korean red chili flakes with earthy, fruity undertones, usually not as spicy as other chili powders.

Kahm yeast. Kahm yeast is a flat, thin, white- to cream-colored powder that tends to grow on the surface of ferments in warmer weather.

Lactic acid. The acid produced by bacteria during fermentation, which stops the growth of harmful bacteria.

Lactic acid bacteria (LAB). Bacteria that produce lactic acid as a byproduct of their metabolism of carbohydrates.

Lactobacillus. A genus of anaerobic rod-shaped bacteria responsible for turning starches and sugars into acids as part of the fermentation process. They are a major part of the LAB group.

Lacto-fermentation. Also called **lactic acid fermentation.** A fermentation method by which vegetables, dairy, and even bread doughs are preserved. Performed primarily by lactic acid bacteria.

Microbiome. A collection of microbes that inhabit a specific environment. Our human microbiome is made up of various smaller microbiomes, such as the gut microbiome, the oral microbiome, and the skin microbiome.

Mold. Mold grows from mold spores that are present everywhere in the air and on the surface of fruits and vegetables. It is raised and fuzzy and can be white, black, blue, green, or even pink.

Pathogenic bacteria. Disease-causing bacteria.

pH. A measure of acidity or alkalinity.

Pickling. The process of preserving foods in an acidic medium.

Prebiotics. Fiber that occurs in a variety of foods and feeds the healthy bacteria already living in your gut.

Probiotics. Microorganisms that are claimed to provide health benefits when consumed.

Salinity. The level of saltiness. The fermentation of sauerkraut best unfolds at a salinity between 1.5% and 2.5%.

SCOBY. A symbiotic culture of bacteria and yeasts. A well-known SCOBY is the cream-colored, mat-like cellulose structure called a *mother*, used as a starter culture for kombucha.

Starter culture. A single bacterial strain or a collection of bacteria used to initiate fermentation. Yogurt is fermented using a starter culture—a dollop of yogurt containing necessary bacteria—from a previous batch. Though unnecessary, some recipes for sauerkraut call for a starter culture, a collection of bacteria commonly present during fermentation.

Tare weight. Tare weight is the weight of an empty container or bowl. Digital scales include a button that resets the scale display when an empty container is placed on the weighing platform, in order to display only the weight of the contents of the container.

Wild fermentation. A fermentation process that relies on naturally present bacteria to initiate fermentation.

About the Author

Holly Howe, a.k.a. the Sauerkraut Wizard, is a fermentation educator and founder of the MakeSauerkraut website.

Since her mid-twenties, Holly has been fascinated by the food she eats and its connection to her health. Holly was compelled to add fermented foods to her family's diet after reading *Nourishing Traditions* by Sally Fallon, a book based on the diets of healthy traditional cultures and the foods they ate. A common thread among these traditional cultures was the inclusion of fermented foods in their diets.

When she first went searching for sauerkraut, Holly found Bubbies sauerkraut at her local health food store and added it to evening meals. As her family reached the bottom of the jar more and more quickly, she soon realized her wallet would be happier if she could cut costs by fermenting her own sauerkraut. And now, over fifteen years later and with hundreds of quarts and dozens of crocks of sauerkraut under her belt, she is helping others bring scrumptious sauerkraut to their dinner tables with her MakeSauerkraut website, local workshops, and now this book.

Not to be stopped with just dill for flavoring sauerkraut (the first flavor she made in her large crock), she has been constantly creating new flavors, which she now shares with you so that you too can effortlessly add the WOW! factor to any meal.

Holly's family lives on Vancouver Island, in beautiful British Columbia. She loves to read and knit by the seaside, hike in the mountains, and bike through the valleys in search of local eateries.

TO LEARN MORE ABOUT HOLLY, VISIT MAKESAUERKRAUT.COM/ABOUT

TO CONTACT HOLLY, PLEASE DROP HER AN EMAIL AT HOLLY@MAKESAUERKRAUT.COM

About MakeSauerkraut

MakeSauerkraut is an online resource run by Holly Howe, a.k.a. the Sauerkraut Wizard. It was founded in 2014 and is growing into a trusted online resource for all things sauerkraut. Holly's goal is to have sauerkraut fermenting in 100,000 homes, one of those homes being yours! Through her passion for fermentation, your eagerness to learn the world's oldest method of preservation and storage, and the help of millions of mighty microbes, we'll get there ... one jar at a time.

The site includes step-by-step instructions for fermenting not only sauerkraut but also pickles, beets, carrots, and coconut water, to name a few. Holly delves deep into everything associated with fermenting vegetables, such as selecting the best fermentation weight, how to slice cabbage, and why weighing your ingredients is so important, along with tips on how to ferment the best batch of sauerkraut.

Since its launch, over 300,000 readers have visited Holly's teaching recipe on making sauerkraut in a jar. Wow!

MAKESAUERKRAUT.COM

Or visit this shortened URL: **fmeasy.me/ms**

What Next?

You now have the information you need to successfully ferment many batches of mouthwatering sauerkraut, effortlessly enjoy them with any meal, and supercharge your gut health as a result.

You are becoming acquainted with our microscopic world, beginning to understand its power, and maybe becoming friends with them.

There is a big, wide world out there when it comes to fermented foods you can easily ferment at home. Here are some recipes on my website to help you take the next step:

5 Simple Fermented Carrot Sticks Recipes
[Crunchy Goodness]

This one is as simple as cutting up carrots and pouring a salty brine over them.

Find the recipe at **fmeasy.me/carrots**

6 Delectable Fermented Beet Recipes
[BODACIOUS!]

Like the carrots, you simply peel and cut up your beets, add some flavoring ingredients, and pour a salty brine over them.

Find the recipe at **fmeasy.me/beets**

Fermented Vegetables Book REVIEW [& Garlic Paste Recipe]

A review of my favorite fermentation book that includes a recipe for garlic paste. Instead of fermenting whole cloves, they are pureed. When finished, garlic paste can be added to any dish to instantly add a mellow garlic flavor.

Find the recipe at **fmeasy.me/garlic**

Fermented Coconut Water [The Complete Guide]

The hardest part of this recipe is getting the kefir grains needed to culture canned coconut water. After that, fermenting coconut water is as easy as opening a can and pouring the coconut water into a jar.

Find the recipe at **fmeasy.me/coconut**

3 Delectable Fermented Cranberry Recipes [Year Round Enjoyment]

The recipe for cranberry relish makes a great addition to any poultry dish and also works as a great addition to an appetizer of crackers and cream cheese. And the Pickled Cranberries truly are a fun snack food and a great conversation starter at any party.

Find the recipe at **fmeasy.me/cranberries**

Traditional Square-Cut Napa Cabbage Kimchi

In this traditional recipe, you soak cut napa cabbage and daikon radish overnight. The cabbage is then drained and mixed with a red pepper seasoning paste made with Korean red pepper powder, fish sauce, salted shrimp and sweet rice-flour porridge. The real thing with more complex flavors than the Kimchi-Style Sauerkraut recipe (pg 116) in this book.

Find the recipe at **fmeasy.me/kimchi**

FREE BOOK BONUS

Free
DOWNLOAD

To download fermentation recipes for Citrus Pickled Red Onions, Cranberry-Orange Relish, Simple Simon Carrot Sticks and Thyme for Leeks Relish, visit this shortened URL: **fmeasy.me/mwsk**

Review Request

5 customer reviews

5.0 out of 5 stars

5 star		100%
4 star		0%
3 star		0%
2 star		0%
1 star		0%

Review this product

Share your thoughts with other customers

Write a customer review

Showing 1-5 of 5 reviews

Top Reviews

Paula M

The BEST book on Fermenting

December 10, 2018

Format: Kindle Edition Verified Purchase

VERY thorough source that dissects a subject in an eas
scientific research and background as to how it benefit
are time & taste tested to perfection! I've made several
because I know they will all be good if Holly has create
provide the reader the opportunity to tweak to their in
more ways to include healthy homemade probiotics int
are. Takes so much of the guesswork out. I've followed
thoroughly enjoyed how much I learned from this extra
at my fingertips now. Her formula for weighing salt ha

If you enjoyed this book or you found it useful, I'd be very grateful if you'd post an honest review on Amazon. Your support really does matter and it really does make a difference. I read all the reviews so I can get your feedback and make changes to the current edition as a result of that feedback.

If you'd like to leave a review, then all you need to do is go to the review section on the book's Amazon page: **fmeasy.me/mwskreview**

Scroll down until you get to the "Customer reviews" section, where you'll see a big button that says "Write a customer review." Click that and you are good to go!

THANK YOU SO MUCH FOR YOUR SUPPORT.

For fabulous ferments and mighty microbes,

Holly Howe

fmeasy.me/mwskreview

Endnotes

1. Vethachai Plengvidhya, Fredrick Breidt Jr., Zhongjing Lu, Henry P. Fleming, "DNA Fingerprinting of Lactic Acid Bacteria in Sauerkraut Fermentations," *Appl. Environ. Microbiol.* 73, no. 23 (Nov 2007): 7697–702, http://aem.asm.org/content/73/23/7697.full

2. O.K. Chun, N. Smith, A. Sakagawa, C.Y. Lee, "Antioxidant Properties of Raw and Processed Cabbages," *Int. J. Food Sci. Nutr.* 55, no. 3 (May 2004): 191–99, https://www.ncbi.nlm.nih.gov/pubmed/15223595

3. K.M. Cho, R.K. Math, S.M. Islam, W.J. Lim, S.Y. Hong, J.M. Kim, M.G. Yun, J.J. Cho, H.D. Yun, "Biodegradation of Chlorpyrifos by Lactic Acid Bacteria during Kimchi Fermentation," *J. Agric. Food Chem.* 57, no. 5 (Mar 2009): 1882–89, https://www.ncbi.nlm.nih.gov/pubmed/19199784

4. Aslan Azizi, "Bacterial-Degradation of Pesticides Residue in Vegetables during Fermentation," in *Pesticides*, ed. Margarita Stoytcheva, (London: IntechOpen, 2011), https://www.intechopen.com/books/pesticides-formulations-effects-fate/bacterial-degradation-of-pesticides-residue-in-vegetables-during-fermentation

5. USDA Food Composition Databases, 2018, https://ndb.nal.usda.gov/ndb/search/list?SYNCHRONIZER_TOKEN=33d79139-0ec9-45d1-842c-7c8a57a7a02e&SYNCHRONIZER_URI=%2Fndb%2Fsearch%2Flist&qt=&ds=&qlookup=sauerkraut+raw&manu=

6. I.H. Choi, J.S. Noh, J.S. Han, H.J. Kim, E.S. Han, Y.O. Song, "Kimchi, a Fermented Vegetable, Improves Serum Lipid Profiles in Healthy Young Adults: Randomized Clinical Trial," *J. Med. Food.* 16, no. 3 (Mar 2013): 223–29, https://www.ncbi.nlm.nih.gov/pubmed/23444963

7. Y. Huang, X. Wang, J. Wang, F. Wu, Y. Sui, L. Yang, Z. Wang, "*Lactobacillus plantarum* Strains as Potential Probiotic Cultures with Cholesterol-Lowering Activity," *J. Dairy Sci.* 96, no. 5 (May 2013): 2746–53, https://www.ncbi.nlm.nih.gov/pubmed/23498020

8. Reuters Health, "Sauerkraut packed with cancer-fighting compounds," CureZone.org, 2002, https://www.curezone.org/art/read.asp?ID=100&db=5&C0=17

9. "Clean 15: EWG's Shopper's Guide to Pesticides in Produce," Environmental Working Group, 2017, https://www.ewg.org/foodnews/clean_fifteen_list.php#.WfICO1u3yUk

Fermentation Made Easy!

MOUTHWATERING SAUERKRAUT FREE BOOK BONUSES

A set of valuable resources and guides
to download, print, and refer to
as you make your first of many batches
of mouthwatering sauerkraut.

1. **My Favorite Sauerkraut-Making Tools & Supplies**
2. **Fermentation Checklist**
3. **Mouthwatering Sauerkraut: A Visual Ingredients Guide**
4. **Bonus Fermentation Recipes**

To download your free set of cheat sheets, visit this shortened URL:

fmeasy.me/mwsk

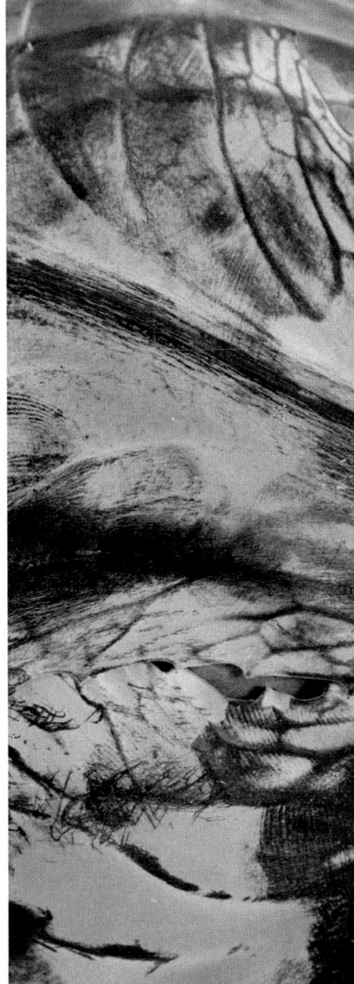